City Improvements, *continued*

Icon	Improvement Name	Building Cost	Maintenance Cost (per turn)	Advances Required
	Palace	200	$0	Masonry
	Power Plant	160	$4	Refining
	Recycling Center	200	$2	Recycling
	SDI Defense	200	$4	Superconductor
	Temple	40	$1	Ceremonial Burial
	University	160	$3	Library Improvement

Spaceship Construction

Unit Name	Resources	Advances Required
Components Propulsion Fuel	160 each	Plastics
Modules Habitation Life Support Solar Panels	320 each	Robotics
Structures	80 each	Space Flight

Computer users are not all alike.
Neither are SYBEX books.

All computer users learn in their own way. Some need straightforward and methodical explanations. Other are just too busy for this approach. But no matter what camp you fall into, SYBEX has a book that can help you get the most out of your computer and computer software while learning at your own pace.

Beginners generally want to start at the beginning. The **ABC's** series, with its step-by-step lessons in plain language, helps you build basic skills quickly. Or you might try our **Quick & Easy** series, the friendly, full-color guide.

The **Mastering** and **Understanding** series will tell you everything you need to know about a subject. They're perfect for intermediate and advanced computer users, yet they don't make the mistake of leaving beginners behind.

If you're a busy person and are already comfortable with computers, you can choose from two SYBEX series—**Up & Running** and **Running Start**. The **Up & Running** series gets you started in just 20 lessons. Or you can get two books in one, a step-by-step tutorial and an alphabetical reference, with our **Running Start** series.

Everyone who uses computer software can also use a computer software reference. SYBEX offers the gamut—from portable **Instant References** to comprehensive **Encyclopedias, Desktop References**, and **Bibles**.

SYBEX even offers special titles on subjects that don't neatly fit a category—like **Tips & Tricks,** the **Shareware Treasure Chests,** and a wide range of books for Macintosh computers and software.

SYBEX books are written by authors who are expert in their subjects. In fact, many make their living as professionals, consultants or teachers in the field of computer software. And their manuscripts are thoroughly reviewed by our technical and editorial staff for accuracy and ease-of-use.

So when you want answers about computers or any popular software package, just help yourself to SYBEX.

For a complete catalog of our publications:

SYBEX Inc.
2021 Challenger Drive, Alameda, CA 94501
Tel: (510) 523-8233/(800) 227-2346 Telex: 336311
SYBEX *Fax: (510) 523-2373*

Civilization
Strategies and Secrets

Civilization
Strategies and Secrets

Jason R. Rich

SYBEX®

San Francisco • Paris • Düsseldorf • Soest

Acquisitions/Developmental Editor: David J. Clark
Editor: Brenda Kienan
Production Editor: Carolina Montilla
Assistant Editors: Abby Azrael, Michelle Nance
Book Designer: Elke Hermanowski
Desktop Production Artist/Icon Designer: Helen Bruno
Reference Charts Designer/Screen Graphics Artist: John Corrigan
Chart Illustrator: Cuong Le
Proofreader/Production Assistant: Elisabeth Dahl
Indexer: Ted Laux
Cover Designer: Ingalls + Associates
Cover Screen Graphic Artist: John Corrigan

Screen reproductions produced with Collage Plus.

Collage Plus is a trademark of Inner Media Inc.

SYBEX is a registered trademark of SYBEX, Inc.

TRADEMARKS: SYBEX has attempted throughout this book to distinguish proprietary trademarks from descriptive terms by following the capitalization style used by the manufacturer.

SYBEX is not affiliated with any manufacturer.

Every effort has been made to supply complete and accurate information. However, SYBEX assumes no responsibility for its use, nor for any infringement of the intellectual property rights of third parties which would result from such use.

Library of Congress Card Number: 93-83897
ISBN: 0-7821-1293-5

Manufactured in the United States of America
10 9 8 7 6 5 4 3 2 1

Acknowledgments

I would like to thank Kathy Gilmore, Terry Haywood, and, of course, Sid Meier at MicroProse Software for their assistance. (Sid, it was a pleasure meeting you in person at CES. You did an incredible job creating this game. Congratulations on its success!)

Also, without the efforts of David Clark and Brenda Kienan at Sybex, this book could never have been published. I greatly appreciate their hard work and interest in this project. Thanks, too, to John Corrigan for special efforts in designing the charts, to Helen Bruno for the art production and icons, to Cuong Le for the chart illustrations, and to Carolina Montilla, Elisabeth Dahl, Abby Azrael, and Michelle Nance.

I'd also like to thank all of the Civilization players who posted their comments on-line through CompuServe, America OnLine, and the MicroProse BBS. Reading their questions, comments, ideas, and concerns about Civilization offered me a guideline for how to best structure this strategy guide.

Civilization is about creating and managing people, so it's only fitting that I mention Victor and Lois Rich, my parents, who created me and my younger sister Melissa. (While I spend my time playing computer and video games, Melissa has a "real job" working long hours at a bank—ha ha!) Thanks also to Mark Giordani and Ellen Bromfield, for their long-time friendship and endless support.

While computer games are fun, it's my family and friends that make life worth living, and no matter how detailed the simulation, no computer could recreate the significance of these people in my life.

Jason R. Rich

Preface

Okay, so you own a personal computer and you were looking for a new way to entertain yourself with it, so you purchased some entertainment software. Out of all the games and simulations currently on the market, you selected Sid Meier's Civilization. Perhaps it was the game's packaging that caught your eye, or maybe you heard about the game from a friend or associate. Whatever the reason, you'll soon discover that you have made an excellent decision.

Unlike many computer games and entertainment packages, Civilization is strategy-based. Civilization contains no fast-paced action, so it does not require lightning reflexes. Instead, this game demands that you think and plan as you take part in simulations that are affected by each choice you make.

Civilization Strategies and Secrets is intended to be your guide as you invent or rewrite history. It provides an introduction and general overview of the game, and offers specific strategies to help you succeed. Novices will find the tutorial chapter invaluable, and more experienced players will value the chapters that provide detailed winning strategies culled from experts who have posted their theories on the various on-line services that have Civilization forums.

You can also use this book as an on-going reference—charts and diagrams that have been included will guide you through the prerequisites to obtaining knowledge and advances that lead to your civilization's ability to build or steal Wonders of the World and other winning elements.

As you will see when you begin to play, Civilization has a very unique user interface, which you must understand. This book contains detailed information to help you.

MicroProse Software currently offers versions of this game for a variety of computer platforms. *Civilization Strategies and Secrets* was written mainly for those using the PC version of the game; however, most of the information (especially the game overview,

Strategy Tips, sample strategies, and reference charts) pertain to all versions currently available.

Civilization is a highly-detailed and somewhat complex game, but this book will give you a quick and easy understanding of the game's operation. As you read *Civilization Strategies and Secrets*, notice the special icons in page margins. These icons are designed to attract your attention to important pieces of information pertaining directly to the game.

The special "Column" icon indicates a Civilization Strategy Tip specifically meant to help you win.

The "Pointing Finger" icon points out Notes—paragraphs that contain cross references, special game techniques, or practical hints for operating the software.

Finally, the "Warning" symbol will alert you to potential problems; things to watch out for while playing Civilization.

These icons, combined with plenty of section headings and graphic screen shots—which were taken from the game itself—should allow you to obtain quickly the information you need and want.

Every effort has been taken to ensure that *Civilization Strategies and Secrets* is the most detailed, easy to understand and complete resource about Civilization on the market. So whether you're a first time player or someone who has already invested a considerable amount of time playing this game, you will find the information within this book extremely useful.

Contents at a Glance

Table of Contents

Chapter 1

Introducing Civilization

Have you ever gotten so involved in a game of Monopoly that it seemed almost real? Monopoly is hardly realistic, but it is easy to become engrossed in the excitement of wheeling and dealing while, for hours, you buy and sell real estate.

Civilization, the game from MicroProse Software, will capture your imagination. Instead of buying and selling real estate, your goal in Civilization is to take a small nomadic tribe of people and do whatever is necessary to expand them into a thriving, space-traveling society. Civilization is not a flashy, action-packed game, nor is it a military shoot'em up game (although you will be forced to protect your people and perhaps enter small battles or even all-out wars). Civilization is a graphics-based, role-playing simulation game—very realistic and highly detailed.

Your Role in Building a Civilization

From the moment the game begins, you will be asked to make decisions that will have ramifications years later. Everything in Civilization is somehow connected—just as it is in real life—and has a cause-and-effect relationship. For example, your tribe of settlers must discover the alphabet before becoming literate. Once the population is literate, your people can then learn about astronomy, which is the first step on the path toward space exploration. Literacy also allows for the opportunity to build a great library and opens the door to developing dozens of other City Improvements (a term that will be explained later in this book).

In Civilization, you must build and control your empire as it comes into contact with other civilizations as well as with small tribes of barbarians. You could find yourself at war with Alexander The Great, or signing some sort of treaty with Napoleon or Caesar. Perhaps you will trade knowledge with Ramses. Just as the game's packaging suggests, in Sid Meier's Civilization you must "Build An Empire To Stand The Test Of Time. The action is simulated, but the excitement is real!"

From the time your civilization is created (around 4000 BC), you are the ruler and decision maker, although you will have Advisors who will offer you suggestions. In the early stages of the game, your job is relatively straightforward. The decisions to be made will be obvious, however, once your civilization expands—you must keep the technological developments and City Improvements moving forward, maintain your military, remember to feed your people, and manage the government and its foreign affairs. These are just a few of the responsibilities that will require you to make choices that will have a direct impact on your civilization's evolution. The key to your civilization's survival is to successfully manage your cities, keep your population happy (or at least content), and make decisions that will benefit your people in both the long term and the short.

Civilization Simulates Historical Events

Civilization is a *simulation*—but what *is* a simulation?

In this case, a simulation is a computer-generated scenario that takes into account a vast amount of fact-based historical information in order to (somewhat) mirror reality. A computer simulation is interactive and open-ended, which means there is no right or wrong direction in which to proceed. There are also very few set rules.

In an arcade game, you must beat one skill level before proceeding to the next. In a simulation, there is a much less predetermined structure. A simulation is a *model*—a representation or replication of something. Pilots use flight simulators to accurately replicate flying airplanes, just as the military uses computer simulations for training. In Civilization, the computer is used to simulate world history. The computer is programmed with an extensive list of cause-and-effect scenarios. Depending on how you proceed and the decisions you make, the programming will automatically adapt your game experience.

Sid Meier, the creator of Civilization, has done extensive research into history to make this game as detailed and realistic as possible; however, as you proceed, your actions may cause your civilization to evolve in different directions than did history, which could lead your civilization to extreme prosperity or to total destruction.

But How Much History Do You Have to Know?

Yes, Civilization is based upon history, however, you don't need to be a history buff to really enjoy this game. In fact, even if you were bored to death in history class, hated reading the textbook, and dreaded those documentary films, you may become obsessed with this game once the civilization you create and manage starts to take shape. Of course, anything you do remember from those history classes may come in handy. However, if you must know any vital historical information, you'll find it outlined within this book, taking a presumably more exciting approach than did your history textbook in high school or college. After all, *this is a game*, so have fun!

The Look and Feel of Civilization

Civilization is primarily a graphics-based game, however, there is little on-screen action (meaning *animated graphics*). The simulation in Civilization is made up of several main information and map screens, which allow you to control the "action" using simple keyboard and/or mouse commands. Use of a mouse is highly recommended, because it will allow you to interact with this game a bit faster. (See Chapter 3, "Installing Civilization," for more details.) It will probably take you an hour or two to become fully acquainted with Civilization and to understand exactly what's happening as you take each turn. Playing the game itself can take between fifteen minutes and fifteen hours, or more, depending on how well-defined and organized your decisions and actions are; so make yourself comfortable at the keyboard and get ready to take on the responsibilities of a ruler.

Civilization: Strategies and Secrets

Your goal is to help your civilization evolve from a small nomadic tribe into a major world power (by eliminating all rival civilizations or by colonizing space).

Scoring Civilization

At the end of each game, a score will be displayed. This score takes into account how well you managed your civilization, based on many criteria, which are described in Chapter 12, "Ending (Winning) the Simulation."

Civilization's Creator Speaks

To get a better understanding of what this game is all about and what actually inspired its creation, check out the interview (in Chapter 2) with Civilization's creator and producer, Sid Meier. Not only will you gain insight into the game, but you might discover a few strategies for getting started.

Winning Civilization

As you proceed, one important key to success is always to look at the big picture. For example, even if you're concentrating on allocating the right resources to defeat attacking barbarians, you must also continue to maintain your civilization through each turn, *and* make the necessary advancements by planning for the future. Thus, you're going to have to accomplish multiple tasks at once, or you will probably fail in the long run. Included within the game is the "Civilopedia," which, along with your Advisors, will offer explanations and key information pertinent to your civilization. You can access the on-screen Civilopedia by holding down the Alt key and pressing C.

Getting Off the Ground

Civilization offers several different pre-game options, which include four major scenario choices:

- Start a New Game
- Load a Saved Game
- EARTH
- Customized World

From here, you must select a difficulty level. Difficulty levels are listed here from the most beginning level to the most advanced:

- Chieftain

- Warlord

- Prince

- King

- Emperor

Needless to say, as a beginner, you'll want to start at the easiest level (as a Chieftain).

You will also have the opportunity to determine how many opponents (additional civilizations) the computer will control within your world—you can choose between three and seven additional civilizations. The fewer civilizations you choose, the greater your opportunity will be to peacefully expand your civilization before having to deal with foreign affairs (alliances, trade, and war).

Each of these choices will be described in Chapter 4 of this book, which offers directions for getting your first civilization off the ground.

Picking Up Tips

As you read this strategy guide, be on the lookout for Strategy Tips, which will be indicated by a special icon (shown here) and will highlight specific strategies or important pieces of information.

Civilization Commands Kudos

Only a handful of computer games offer open-ended game play experience and detail equal to Civilization. When you see, first-hand, just how incredible this game is, you won't be surprised to learn that Civilization has won the Software Publishers Association's Critics' Choice Award for "Best Consumer Product," "Best Strategy Program," and "Best Entertainment Program."

MicroProse's president and CEO, Bill Stealey, has commented, "In computer entertainment, these awards are like the Oscars. To be nominated for one is exciting. To be nominated in three categories is an honor. But to sweep the three categories in which we were nominated is phenomenal—like hitting a grand slam in the World Series!"

The positive reviews keep coming in. In the May 1992 issue of Omni magazine, computer game reviewer Gregg Keizer reported, "Computer simulations may sound oh-so-serious, but the best are as fun to play as any head-bashing video game....You won't find a more entertaining simulation on the shelves this year."

Have a Winning Reign

As you play Civilization, you will be experiencing one of the best simulation games the computer software industry has to offer. Your imagination, along with your ability to keep in mind the bigger picture, will play a key role in your success as the ruler of your civilization. Enjoy your reign, and good luck.

Chapter 2

The Inside Scoop

Sid Meier, the co-founder of MicroProse Software, is the man behind Civilization's creation and success. Sid has made a career of creative computer game design, with innovative new ideas for improving the overall quality of interactive games. From his office in Hunt Valley, Maryland, Sid spent a few minutes talking about himself and his game, Civilization.

Interview with Sid Meier

Question: *How did you get involved in the computer game business?*

SID MEIER: Well, I studied computers in college and started with a more mainstream computing job. Shortly after that, personal computers came out, which gave me a chance to combine computers—which was my job—with my fascination for games, which I have enjoyed playing since I was a kid. I started to write computer games for fun on the Atari 800 computer—that led to writing games for commercial distribution. A bit later, my partner and I founded MicroProse Software.

Question: *How did the idea for Civilization evolve?*

SID MEIER: We created Railroad Tycoon previously, and liked the way its features turned out. The concept in that game was to build and maintain a working railroad system. You started with a little seed and built it into something much bigger. Railroad Tycoon allowed excellent interaction between the various elements of the game—you had to wear a number of different hats while playing. For example, you had to build stuff, operate what you built, and finance it. Whatever you did in one area of the game influenced the other areas, so you were always kept occupied.

When we finished Railroad Tycoon, we started looking for other game ideas with these qualities. We looked at existing games—like Empire, SimCity, and Populous—and figured out what we would have done differently to make these popular games better.

Between what we learned from Railroad Tycoon and from evaluating other games, we came up with the concept for a game that involved conquering the world and journeying through time. We put together a prototype, and from the early stages, Civilization was fun to play.

Question: How long did it take to create Civilization?

SID MEIER: At MicroProse, our development methodology is to quickly put together a model so we obtain the general feel for the game, then go back and add more and more stuff as we play the model and discover what we like and don't like about it. Civilization was one of the few games that turned out pretty much as we originally envisioned it. The actual development process took just under three years, but we took a break during that time to finish Covert Action. The whole process took about a year-and-a-half.

Most of the time, it was co-producer Bruce Shelley and myself working on the game. Toward the end, we had about fifteen artists and musicians adding their talents to the original PC version of Civilization.

Question: How much previous historical knowledge is required to play Civilization?

SID MEIER: Very little. We did some historical research, but we tried to use knowledge that we already had. We relied on the assumption that people who played the game would have similar basic historical knowledge. We didn't want to create a game that depended on learning a lot of historical background information from the game's manual or another book. A game based on a lot of research or on a lot of knowledge will only appeal to a small group of people—or historians.

Question: What was the biggest obstacle you had to overcome in creating Civilization?

SID MEIER: It took us a while to find the right approach. Early on, Civilization had a more SimCity [Maxis Software] approach, where some things happened automatically. This method didn't give the player enough control, so we went with using different types of units [Editor's Note: In Civilization, every active member of the population—settlers, diplomats, etc.—is represented as an individual graphic icon, called a unit] which the player could create and then manage. Initially, the map structure of Civilization was much bigger, and the time units were smaller, which made the entire game somewhat overwhelming.

We then had to modify the game and figure out what a reasonable amount of game play time for Civilization was. We also had to balance the military, political, and economic systems. Originally, the military aspect of the game was dominant.

Question: *How long should a typical simulation take?*

SID MEIER: We figure that you'll want to accomplish quite a bit in an evening, and that most people aren't going to spend more than three or four evenings at a time playing out a simulation.

Based on this, we created a game in which each simulation takes between ten and twenty hours to complete. Of course, how long a simulation takes is based upon how well you play and what developments take place.

Question: *How did you select the various Advancements and City Improvements that are incorporated into the game?*

SID MEIER: The important thing about this aspect of the game is that each Advancement or City Improvement leads to the creation of something else you can use.

Early on in the game's development, I picked out about fifty things I thought would make good icons to represent progress during the game. As it turns out, we used many of the Advancements and City Improvements that were on my original list.

When you pick an Advancement or City Improvement, it offers a specific benefit to your civilization. By selecting what technologies you go after, you can steer your civilization toward whatever your goals happen to be.

Question: What key elements do you feel make up a good game?

SID MEIER: There are a couple of things we do to ensure that we produce good games. First, we play our own games continuously throughout the development process. If we're not having fun playing a game that is in development, we fix it as early as possible.

We also make sure that it's not just the game's designer who is having fun, or simply that the computer is showing off its graphics capabilities. The player is the central character, and we take every step possible to ensure that the game is designed for the player. The player should be totally involved in the game.

Question: What would you say is the most difficult part of playing Civilization?

SID MEIER: I'd have to say that Civilization is one of the few games for which the learning curve is pretty good. The game starts out easy and gradually gives you more and more to do.

In Civilization, you must spend some time early on learning the interface and where certain pieces of information are. It is important that you understand the general idea of the game, which is that you must build and expand your civilization from the beginning.

If you start the game and just wander around to see what happens, not too much will happen. This type of game depends on you, the player, to make things happen. You are the star, and you must build cities and create a civilization, with the idea that bigger is better.

Question: What should first-time Civilization players be on the lookout for?

SID MEIER: Once again, the key is to explore. Beyond the idea of building cities and expanding, I think we really want you to try achieving different goals each time you play. Try being a military leader one time and a peaceful leader the next time. Perhaps you'll attempt to build a civilization that is an economic superpower, or extremely advanced, by making your goal to achieve as many Advancements and technologies as possible.

The first time you play, definitely select the Chieftain [beginner] level. Other than that, play Civilization the way you want to play, and define your own goals. Be creative and have fun with your exploration.

Question: Do you have any other advice?

SID MEIER: I would suggest that the first time you play, you should sit down with someone else who has already played Civilization and understands how the game works. At any time, it is always fun to play with someone else so that you can discuss things as you go.

This game does not have a right way or a wrong way to play it. Don't be afraid to try things. If your civilization is ruthlessly crushed, re-boot the computer and start again.

Question: What is the future of Civilization? Will there be a sequel?

SID MEIER: We don't have any definite plans for a sequel, although it does seem like we should do *something*—this game has a large following. I'd like to take the basic concept and create another fun-to-play game, as opposed to adding a few new maps to the existing game.

Right now, we are adapting the existing Civilization game to other platforms. In addition to [the version] available for the PC, there is a recently-released Apple Macintosh version, and an Amiga version. In late 1993, we'll also be releasing a special Windows version, which will take advantage of the high-resolution graphics available to PC-based computer users who operate under Windows.

Our goal when we adapt Civilization to another computer platform or operating system is to keep the game play the same, but to improve upon the quality of the graphics, whenever possible.

Chapter 3

Installing Civilization

Before you play Civilization, you must install and configure the program to your particular computer. This chapter will tell you how.

Civilization for the PC

Civilization is now available for the Apple Macintosh and Commodore Amiga as well as the PC. A separate version is also under development (for release in 1994) for the Super Nintendo Entertainment System. Basic game play in all of these versions is supposed to be identical, but the graphics will look somewhat different, depending on the version.

Civilization Strategies and Secrets offers strategies that can be used when playing the game on any of these systems, however, all screen shots and game play research has been done on the PC version. Also, in the installation section of this book, we're going to concentrate on the PC version.

What You Get and What You Need

You can purchase the PC edition of Civilization on either 5¼" disks or 3½" disks—check the side panel of the packaging to make sure you're getting the correct disk size. Civilization will run on an IBM PC, XT, or AT; a Tandy 1000; a Compaq; or a 100% IBM-compatible computer; with at least 640K RAM (random access memory).

Mouse or Keyboard Options

On the PC, the entire game can be controlled using just the keyboard; however, using a mouse is strongly recommended, as it gives you additional flexibility throughout the game.

Graphics Capabilities

Civilization is compatible with these graphics controllers:

- IBM EGA
- IBM MCGA
- IBM VGA
- Tandy 1000 graphics system

If you're running the software in EGA mode, you must have at least 256K on the graphics card. The better the graphics capabilities of your computer, the more detailed each screen will be when you begin the simulation.

Civilization runs under IBM or Microsoft DOS, version 3.0 or higher. A special Windows version is also available.

Stimulate Your Senses with Sound

The human body (like the one you are living in) has several senses—sight, smell, touch, taste, and hearing. You can't touch or taste a computer game (*unless you literally take a* "byte" *out of your disks*), and the computer doesn't have a smell, so you must depend on your other senses to get a sense of realism, while relying on your imagination to compensate for what's lacking.

In addition to a visual presentation (on the screen), Civilization provides for your ability to hear sounds and even background music in certain scenes.

Civilization's Sound Capabilities

This software is compatible with a variety of sound boards, but you can also just take advantage of your PC's built-in sound capabilities by selecting IBM Sound at the appropriate menu when the game begins.

If you are using a Tandy computer with the Tandy music chip, for improved sound and music, you can use the Tandy Sound option. Civilization works well with the AdLib/Sound Blaster (or another compatible board), or the Roland MT-32 MIDI board. For other sound boards, you can also use a custom sound board driver available from MicroProse software or the sound board's manufacturer.

Your computer has a built-in speaker, but its capabilities are limited. Thus, the folks at MicroProse have made Civilization compatible with several popular sound boards.

Sound Board Compatibility

Creative Labs offers several models of their popular sound boards, which have just about become a standard within the PC industry. These sound boards are available from your local computer dealer.

The original Sound Blaster, which sells for approximately $150, can deliver all of the audio power built into thousands of games and applications, including Civilization. This optional half-height card fits within your computer and offers an eleven-voice FM music synthesizer, 8-bit digitized voice channel input and output, a joystick port, built-in power amplifier (so the board can connect directly to stereo headsets, speakers, or a home entertainment/stereo system), a MIDI interface, and the necessary software drivers to operate the board with your computer. The Sound Blaster will fit into any of your computer's 8-bit expansion slots.

If you really want to take advantage of your computer's sound capabilities, the Sound Blaster Pro Basic, which sells for approximately $230, offers additional features, such as: stereo audio output, a CD-ROM interface, multiple audio inputs, and enhanced bundled software. Creative Labs also offers the Sound Blaster Pro and the Sound Blaster 16 ASP sound boards.

Dozens of other companies also manufacture less expensive yet totally compatible sound boards that will work with Civilization. If you want a board to work with Civilization, just be sure it is compatible with the Sound Blaster or Roland MT-32 MIDI boards—that will mean it's also compatible with Civilization.

Running the Game from Floppy Disks

It is possible to run Civilization from floppy disks, however, hard disk installation is recommended, in order to avoid having to swap disks during game play. To run the software from floppies, make copies of the original (distribution) disks using the DOS command, Copy. You'll need a set of floppies—one blank disk (either 5¼" or 3½") for each of the distribution disks, plus an extra blank disk on which to store your game data. After you have formatted your blank disks,

1. Insert the first Civilization distribution disk in drive A:, and a blank disk into drive B:.

2. At the A:\ prompt, type: **COPY A:*.* B:** and press Enter (Return). (This will work even if your computer has only one disk drive.)

You'll need to repeat this procedure to copy each of the game's distribution disks onto a second set of floppies. When you're ready to run the game,

1. Insert Civilization Disk #1 into drive A:.

2. At the A:\ prompt, type: **CIV** and press Enter. The computer will run the game from the floppy disk.

During the installation and/or game play process, you may be asked to insert other Civilization disks, which will be requested by number (for example, Civilization Disk #2). If you have two floppy disk drives, you can begin the game by inserting Disk #1 in drive A: and Disk #2 in drive B:. Do not remove the disks from the drives unless you are prompted to do so.

If your computer has a built-in Turbo mode, be sure that you have set your computer to operate at its normal speed before you run Civilization. If you don't do this, the game may crash.

Installing and Running the Game from a Hard Disk

If you have a hard disk in your computer, you'll have to run the Install Civilization program, which will be found on Disk #1. To do this,

1. Place Disk #1 into your A: drive.

2. At the A:\ DOS prompt, type: **INSTALLC** and press Enter.

Using its own internal batch files, the Civilization program will create a subdirectory called MPS (MicroProse Software), and then, within that directory, create a subdirectory called CIV, into which the game will be copied.

Once the software is installed (it's pretty much a self-installing program), to run Civilization,

1. At the C:\ prompt, type: **CD \MPS** and press Enter.

2. A C:\MPS\ prompt will appear. Type: **CIV** and press Enter to run the program.

If your hard disk is named something other than C: (drive D:, E:, etc.), type INSTALL, followed immediately by the drive letter—for example, **INSTALLD**—and press Enter.

Your computer should not be running any memory-resident programs or utilities when you install or run Civilization. If your computer is running other programs, they could conflict with Civilization and cause both programs to *hang*, or not install correctly.

If you try to install the game and an on-screen message appears indicating a lack of memory, try installing the game using EGA graphics instead of VGA graphics. Using the IBM Sounds option (as opposed to the Sound Blaster driver or another sound board driver) also requires less memory.

Civilization's Copy Protection

For your convenience, the Civilization distribution disks are not copy-protected. This means that you can freely make backup copies for your own use. It does not mean that you can legally make copies for the use of other people.

Pirating and distributing commercial software to others without written permission is illegal. To help protect itself from people copying and distributing illegal copies of the software, MicroProse has incorporated a copy-protection scheme into the game.

Fifty turns or so after the game begins, you will be asked a question, shown a graphic icon (on the screen), and provided with page numbers, as shown in Figure 3.1.

To continue playing the game, you must have the original Civilization owner's manual at your disposal. You'll have to:

1. Locate the pages in the manual that are described on the game screen, then match up the graphic icon on the screen

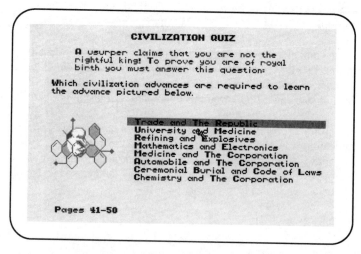

Figure 3.1: To continue the game, you must answer correctly whatever Civilization Quiz Question is posed

with the one found on the lower-left corner of the page in the manual.

2. Near the graphic icon in the manual, in parentheses, two advances will be listed. Back on the computer screen there will be a list of choices. Match the advances described in the game's manual with the correct choices on the screen.

3. If the match is correct, the game will continue. If you select the wrong choice from the menu, you'll be given a second chance to answer correctly. If you blow it twice, the computer will assume you are using an illegal copy of the game and the simulation will end.

Answering the copy protection question should take no more than thirty seconds if you have access to the game's manual.

Upgrading Civilization

Since Civilization's first introduction in late 1991, the folks at MicroProse Software have made a few upgrades to the software. These upgrades are available to be downloaded, free of charge, from MicroProse's 24-hour BBS service, or from commercial on-line services that offer a computer gaming forum, such as CompuServe and America On-line.

When you download an upgrade file, such as CIVV05.ZIP, you'll need a decompression program to expand the compressed file. PKunzip, a popular decompression program, is available as shareware, meaning that you can obtain the program from a friend or electronic bulletin board, but to use the program beyond the initial trial period, you have to register and pay a small fee for it. Other popular decompression programs, such as LHarc and Unzip, are in the public domain, meaning anyone can freely distribute and use them.

Follow the instructions for the decompression program you're using, and after decompression is complete, copy all of the .EXE files to C:\MPS\CIV on your hard disk, or to the main program disk if you're running from floppies.

To determine whether you have the most up-to-date version of Civilization, check with MicroProse Software's technical support people by calling or posting e-mail on CompuServe or the MicroProse BBS, or ask a knowledgeable salesclerk at the location where you purchased your computer software. Ask about the number of the most recent version released, and compare it to the version number listed on your game's setup title screen.

Your Reign Is About to Begin

Civilization is a complex game with many different variables— population management, military strategy, financial planning, and more. For a general overview of key aspects, read Chapters 4, 5, and 6. Then you should feel comfortable enough with the game to explore for yourself. Later chapters will provide you with a resource for developing strategies and overcoming the various obstacles that your civilization may encounter.

Chapter 4

Civilization Basics

Let's Get Your Simulation Started

Now that the Civilization software is installed on your computer, it's time to start your simulation. Assuming you're running the software from a hard disk, at the C:\MPS prompt type: **CIV**. Press Enter and the simulation will run.

Civilization's Pre-Game Options

Before the game itself actually begins, several pre-game options are presented to you, including the graphic and sound driver selection menus, along with the skill level option.

Selecting a Graphics Mode

First, you can select the graphics mode under which Civilization will be running. The Graphic Driver menu appears just below the center of the game's title screen (as shown in Figure 4.1) and will provide you with four choices:

- VGA (256 colors)
- MCGA (256 colors)
- EGA (16 colors)
- Tandy 1000 (16 colors)

Enter the appropriate selection (based on your hardware configuration) and press Enter. If you are using a laptop or notebook computer with an LCD display, selecting EGA should allow Civilization to operate correctly. For full-size computers with color or monochrome monitors, make your selection based on the type of monitor and graphics card you are using.

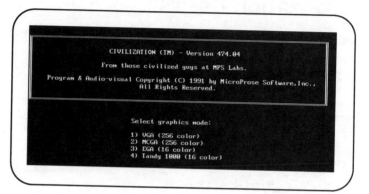

Figure 4.1: Select the right graphics mode for your computer

Selecting a Sound Mode

Next, you will be prompted to select the sound mode for the simulation. If you're going to be playing in an office situation, you'll probably want to select the No Sounds Please option, so that you can play the game quietly. If you're an avid computer game player, you may have invested already in a sound board—a wonderful enhancement to any computer games system.

Using Sound Boards and Drivers   Civilization is compatible with the AdLib/Sound Blaster, which is probably the most popular optional sound board available. As you'll see in Figure 4.2, Civilization also works with the Roland MT-32 MIDI board, or can be modified to accept custom drivers. If you're going to be using a custom sound driver, check with the folks at MicroProse (or the sound board's manufacturer) to determine compatibility.

Choosing the IBM Sounds Option   Finally, if you have not yet invested in a sound board, you'll probably want to select the IBM Sounds option, which takes advantage of your computer's built-in speaker(s).

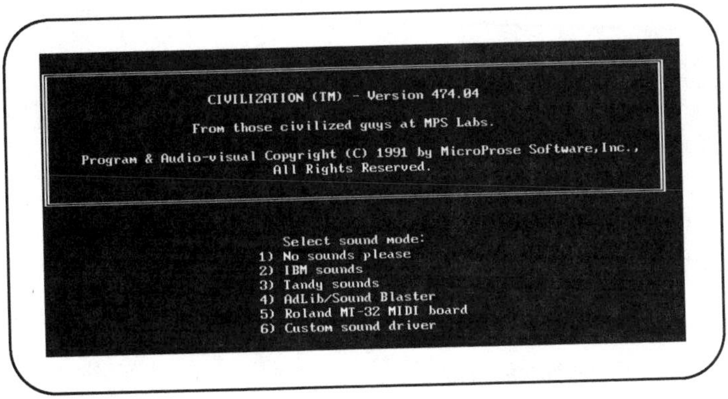

```
        CIVILIZATION (TM) - Version 474.04

        From those civilized guys at MPS Labs.

Program & Audio-visual Copyright (C) 1991 by MicroProse Software,Inc.,
                All Rights Reserved.



                Select sound mode:
              1) No sounds please
              2) IBM sounds
              3) Tandy sounds
              4) AdLib/Sound Blaster
              5) Roland MI-32 MIDI board
              6) Custom sound driver
```

Figure 4.2: Select the sound driver to be used with Civilization

Mouse Play or Keyboard Play

After you have made your selection from the Sound Options menu, the next option menu—the Mouse/Keyboard Drivers menu—will appear, asking you to define how you will be interacting with the game. This menu offers only two choices:

- Mouse and Keyboard

- Keyboard Only

Option one, Mouse and Keyboard, should be selected if you're going to be using a mouse along with the computer keyboard—which is highly recommended, because the mouse allows you to interact faster and more easily with the game. Perhaps you're one of those PC owners who hasn't yet discovered why using a mouse is helpful, so you don't own one. No problem—either run to your local computer store and pick up a mouse, or select option two, Keyboard Only, then press Enter. The Mouse/Keyboard drivers menu is shown in Figure 4.3. You make your selection by pressing 1 or 2; it is not necessary to press Enter.

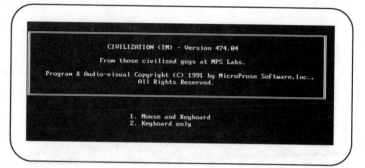

CIVILIZATION (TM) - Version 474.04
From those civilized guys at MPS Labs.
Program & Audio-visual Copyright (C) 1991 by MicroProse Software,Inc.,
All Rights Reserved.

1. Mouse and Keyboard
2. Keyboard only

Figure 4.3: Select Mouse and/or Keyboard drivers

Automatic Loading of Drivers

Now Civilization will load automatically the appropriate *drivers*, which are special programming subroutines that allow Civilization to operate correctly with your computer hardware. A message— One Moment Please—should appear briefly on the computer screen. The simulation will begin soon after. As you are transported into a computer-generated world, the game screen will go blank, followed by a screen listing the game's copyright credits. Then the message, A MicroProse Presentation, will be displayed, followed by a list of the key people involved in production of the game.

If you don't want to watch the game's credits, press the space bar and the main title screen will appear.

Starting a Simulation

On the lower portion of the main title screen (shown in Figure 4.4) is a menu found in a small box. From this menu, you can now select the type of simulation with which you wish to experiment. The main options include:

- Start a New Game
- Load a Saved Game

Figure 4.4: The Title screen menu

- EARTH
- Customized World

Starting a New Game

The Start a New Game option begins a new simulation—in the year 4000 BC, on a world much like Earth. Unless you achieve your ultimate goals—to conquer the world and/or colonize space—the game will eventually conclude in the following years, depending on which skill level you choose:

Chieftain	2100 AD
Warlord	2080 AD
Prince	2060 AD
King	2040 AD
Emperor	2020 AD

We'll talk more about choosing skill levels later in this chapter.

As you become good at Civilization, a typical "quick game" could take several hours to play, so you'll probably want to save the game, take a break, and continue playing at a later time. (Directions for saving the game data are outlined later in this book.)

Start a New Game can be used to provide a tutorial overview of the Civilization. This will be demonstrated in Chapter 7.

Resuming a Saved Game

Load a Saved Game can be used to recover a simulation that you have saved and stopped playing for a while. After you select Load a Saved Game, you will be asked to identify the disk drive on which your saved game data is stored, and then a menu will appear listing ten saved games (or, if you used AutoSave, you will see as many as ten *portions* of the same game). Highlight and select the saved game (or portion of a game) you want to resume.

Choosing to Play on Earth

Selecting the EARTH option from this menu allows you to experience a simulation that takes place on the planet Earth. In this case, your adversaries will be computer-controlled tribes, located on their historically correct continents.

Customizing Your World

Should you choose Customized World, you will have the opportunity to play "God" by creating your own planet from scratch. Before this simulation begins, you actually must create the land mass (on screen, of course), determine average temperatures, specify how much moisture is available, and choose a starting date from additional menus, as seen in Figure 4.5. Keep in mind that the choices you make now will form a basis for how your simulation progresses. When you alter the climate of a continent, for example, there are bound to be drastic changes in how the people on that continent evolve.

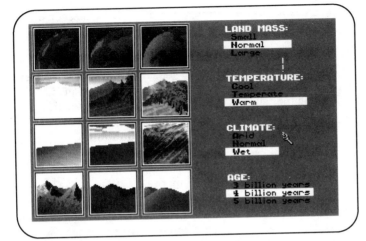

Figure 4.5: The Customized World options

In the subsequent menus under the Customized World option, use the *middle* choice on each menu screen to create a world that is more similar to Earth.

Viewing the Civilization Hall of Fame

Civilization automatically stores the top five most prosperous civilizations that have been created by players. When View Hall of Fame is selected from the main menu, information about these top-ranked civilizations is displayed. After you view these historical records, press Enter and the game's main menu will once again appear. The Hall of Fame is provided for your information only; you don't get to choose to play a Hall of Fame simulation, but must set up your own.

Civilization's Story

Once you have defined the simulation you wish to play, the story behind Civilization is displayed automatically on screen. Like any epic adventure, this story begins, "In the beginning...." The story explains how the Earth was created, and then basically posts a job opening for you to fill—for the great leader of the civilization which is about to form, of course.

The story takes a few minutes to scroll through, so be patient. In the future, if you're comfortable tinkering with computer files, you can use your word processor or text editor to modify the Civilization file called STORY.TXT and edit this story, making it a bit shorter or more to your liking.

Modifying Text Files

Just about any of the Civilization .TXT files (which contain the text you see during the game) can be modified. Before editing a .TXT file, however, you should first copy the existing file onto a blank disk so that you have an extra backup copy. Remember, too, that you can change the text but can*not* change the formatting of the existing text or erase any of the file's syntax, or the game may not be able to read the .TXT file correctly.

You can use your printer to create a hard copy of the text files that make up the Civilopedia (which will be described in detail in Chapter 5). This will make it easier to refer to the Civilopedia while playing the game. The .TXT files that make up the "Civilopedia" include: BLURB0.TXT, BLURB1.TXT and BLURB4.TXT.

In addition to STORY.TXT, other files can be edited as well, which allows you to further customize the game. You can add a touch of humor, if you like.

If, as ruler, you also want to play newspaper editor, you can edit the KING.TXT file, which contains the newspaper headlines you'll see throughout the game. Before editing this file, though, you should probably play the game for a while to determine exactly what each of the headlines mean.

Selecting a Skill Level

After you have read the story about how the planet was created, you must select the level of difficulty for the upcoming simulation (see

Figure 4.6). There are five levels of difficulty to choose from:

- Chieftain (the easiest level)
- Warlord
- Prince
- King
- Emperor (the most difficult level)

The Beginning Level: Chieftain

As a beginner, you will definitely want to experience your first simulation as a Chieftain. In this level, information windows will appear during the game to offer you playing advice. The primary differences between each level involve how long it takes for advancements to occur, and how long it takes to produce new units. (In Civilization, every citizen is a settler, military, or diplomatic "*unit.*")

Levels also differ in how easy it is to maintain the happiness of your people and to avoid civil disorder. At lower levels than King,

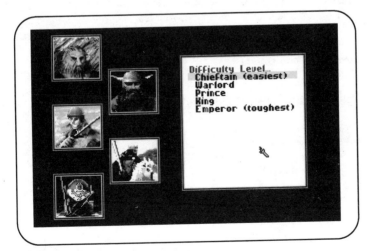

Figure 4.6: The Level of Difficulty menu

your opponents will not be evenly matched to you in capabilities, so you'll have a small advantage, and you should be able to evolve more quickly.

More Advanced Levels:
Warlord, Prince, King, and Emperor

As a **Warlord**, you'll find that your rivals will be a bit more difficult to defeat and technology will take a bit longer to acquire. Opponents will be more skilled than those you encountered as a Chieftain, but you'll still have the advantage.

Just as you would expect, the **Prince** level is even more difficult than the Warlord level, but your opponents are still not evenly matched with your civilization, so you can have the upper hand.

Should you decide to experience a simulation as a **King**, you're going to have to work hard to keep your people happy. You'll also need to become a superior military planner when it comes to defeating your opponents (who will not be evenly matched with you).

Finally, as an **Emperor**, MicroProse reports that the game *can* be won—but if you choose this option, your leadership skills will be put to the ultimate test as you attempt to keep everything proceeding forward in order to colonize space before your enemies attack and defeat your civilization.

Selecting the Level of Competition

As your civilization expands, you will meet other civilizations and tribes, as well as barbarians—you're going to have to fight them or sign peace treaties to co-exist on the planet. After selecting the skill level at which you'll play, you're going to have to select the Level of Competition, which means determining the number of opposing civilizations and tribes (between three and seven) you're going to meet as your simulation progresses (see Figure 4.7).

If you choose a large number of civilizations, it doesn't mean necessarily that you're going to be attacked from all sides by

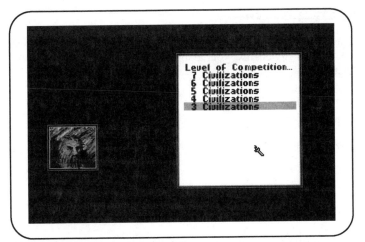

Figure 4.7: Select the number of opponent civilizations

different enemies (although sudden attacks are *always* possible). It does, however, mean that as you expand, you're going to meet your neighbors a bit faster, so you'll have to deal with them earlier in the game (maybe right at the start). Once you've progressed a bit, contact with other civilizations can give you advantages in the ability to open trade routes and develop allies. War isn't always necessary, nor is it always preferred. Civilization is not a military-based game; however, every civilization is constantly faced with the possibility of war.

During the game, you may have to make multiple decisions at once. For example, you may need to decide whether to expand your civilization by creating new cities or attacking others, or to make your existing civilization stronger from an internal standpoint.

If you're torn between expanding your civilization and protecting your cities, always protect what already exists. Should you expand too quickly, you won't be able to protect yourself against multiple attacks or sudden internal problems, such as civil unrest. Whenever possible, upgrade existing cities with new technological advances and maybe even a few luxuries.

Choosing Your Tribe

Now you choose which tribe you want to lead. If you have chosen to have three opponents, your choices for the tribe you lead will include:

- Roman
- Babylonian
- German
- Russian
- Zulu
- French

If you have chosen to have seven opponents, you can add to your choices for the tribe you lead:

- Egyptian
- American
- Greek
- Indian
- Aztec
- Chinese
- English
- Mongol

From a game play standpoint, it doesn't matter which tribe you choose, unless you selected the EARTH game option, which places your tribe and your rival civilizations in their historically correct geographical location.

Naming Yourself Great Leader

Finally, a dialog box will appear, where you must enter your name (or pseudonym), which can be up to fourteen characters long. If you choose not to enter your name, the computer will provide you with one, directly from history, that it feels is suitable.

Once your name is identified, a screen like that shown in Figure 4.8 will appear. Your name will appear as the leader of the tribe you have selected. Be sure to note the technological advances your tribe already holds. You may want to check the Technological Advancement charts later in this book to determine the best tracks to follow in terms of your tribe's future advancements.

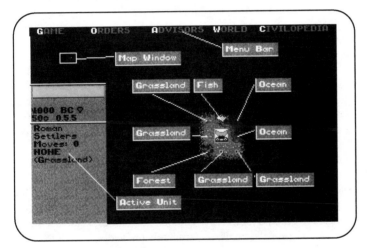

Figure 4.8: The Main Game screen

Defining Short-Term Goals

At the start of the game, you control a group of Settlers, who are wandering in search of a location in which to settle. Your immediate goals in the game are:

1. To help your people form a capital city

2. To enable them to protect the city

3. To enable them to feed themselves

Selecting the Location of Your Capital City

In your next decision, the most important one you've made thus far, you must choose an appropriate location for the capital city you'll be founding.

In Civilization, geographical area has a major impact on your people's productivity and overall welfare. Just as in real life, a Civilization city must have some natural resources to use, for agricultural and industrial growth occur both in the long and short terms.

When you are searching for a good location, use common sense. Rivers allow for easy irrigation, which means agriculture will be strong and, initially, your people will be fed. Grasslands are also good for agriculture. As you expand, you might want to look for hills to construct cities near—hills are excellent for mining, which leads to earning extra funds. Mountains offer good protection for cities.

Don't forget—it is possible to convert squares of one type of land into another type of land, but this takes time and resources. For example, forests can be converted into plains, and grasslands can be converted into forests, based on your needs. Always be on the lookout for graphic icons that symbolize resources, such as fish in the water or animals, gems, and minerals on land.

At first, you'll know little about the terrain around you. As you explore, the blackness on the screen and on the maps will slowly disappear.

Determining the best site for your capital city may take a bit of exploring. But until your city is founded, your unprotected group of wandering settlers is vulnerable to attack. If, at the Level of Competition menu, you selected a large number of other civilizations, you can't spend a lot of time wandering around, or you may immediately encounter an invading enemy. If this happens, your civilization will crumble right away.

When playing at easier levels, or with fewer other existing civilizations, take up to six or eight turns to explore the terrain and establish your capital city. At more difficult levels, or when playing with many other existing civilizations, you'll want to form your capital city immediately.

If you're playing as a Chieftain, the easiest level, windows will appear, offering suggestions for good locations.

Once you have found a perfect location for your capital city, you'll need to issue your first Orders. To do this, you'll use the Orders pull-down menus at the top of the game screen.

When you first establish your city, your people will governed by Despotism (which means you are the sole ruler with total power). See the section on governments in Chapter 7 for additional details on the six types of governments available within a simulation.

To protect your city, use at least two Militia units. To do this, first create the units by selecting the Change option in the City screen. As each unit is created, fortify it by choosing the Fortified option from the Orders pull-down menu.

Later you'll want to protect your city with Phalanx units (stronger and more advanced than Militia units), which can be done once you have discovered Bronze Working.

Once the capital city is established and protected, it's time to start exploring and expanding. To do this, you must create additional military units to explore and to create additional cities by creating Settler units.

From this point on, everything you do will be done in *turns*. Each turn represents the passage of time; at the beginning of each turn, you make your decisions. Often, you'll need to accomplish multiple tasks during a single turn, which makes it vital that you understand what everything on the game screen represents—the game screens are covered in the next chapter.

Chapter 5

Understanding the Game Screens

Civilization has two primary game screens:

- The Main Game screen
- The City screen

The Main Game screen (see Figure 5.1) offers a close-up graphical overview of the terrain in the center of the screen, a series of pull-down menu options at the top of the screen, a small map of the entire (explored) world, and a data window containing vital information about each terrain square, city, and active unit.

The City screen also includes a set of pull-down menu options, and graphically depicts within its windows just about everything you need to know about a specific city within your civilization: its location, and information about its population, resources, food storage, obtained improvements, and more.

The Main Game Screen

At the top of the Main Game screen there are five primary pull-down menus. They are:

- The Game menu
- The Orders menu
- The Advisors menu
- The World menu
- The Civilopedia menu

To activate any of these pull-down menus (one at a time) hold down the Alt key on the keyboard and press the first letter of the key word—Game, Orders, Advisors, World, or Civilopedia—seen on the screen (i.e. Alt+G for the Game menu, Alt+O for the Orders menu, and so on). If you're using a mouse, you can point the mouse

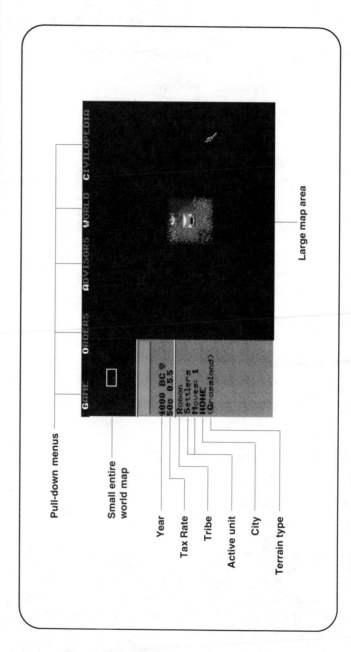

Pull-down menus

Small entire
world map

Year

Tax Rate

Tribe

Active unit

City

Terrain type

Large map area

Figure 5.1: The Main Game screen as it appears at the beginning of a game

at the appropriate choice on the menu bar and click to select that choice.

Within each pull-down menu is a variety of options, some of which you will use often. Others you'll use less frequently, but when you do use them, they can be extremely helpful.

Using the Game Menu

By pressing Alt+G or clicking the mouse on the word Game, you will discover the following choices in the Game pull-down menu (as seen in Figure 5.2):

- Tax Rate
- Luxuries Rate
- Find City
- Options
- Save Game
- Revolution
- Retire
- QUIT to DOS

Tax Rates and Luxury Rates

In order to make internal improvements and expand, you're going to need finances. The Tax Rate option allows you to determine what percentage of your people's income will go toward the upkeep of the civilization. When you select this option, a submenu will appear in another window (Figure 5.3), offering you multiple Tax Rate options. From the start of a simulation, the default Tax Rate is 50% Tax (50% Science) and the default Luxury Rate is 0% Luxuries (50% Science).

One of your toughest goals as you proceed in this game will be to keep your citizens happy. To do this, you'll need to allocate resources to create luxuries. One way to keep your people happy is to

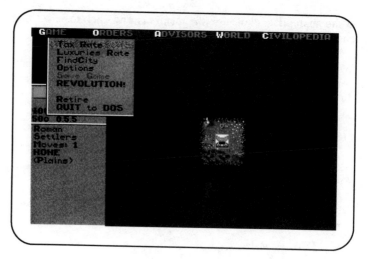

Figure 5.2: The Main Game screen, showing the Game menu

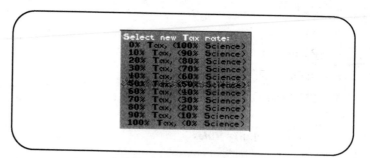

Figure 5.3: The Tax Rate menu, found under the Game menu

offer them a high Luxuries Rate, which means that a large portion of the city's tax income will be sent to build luxury items for the population. When you select this option, a submenu will appear offering you a variety of Luxury Rate levels.

Making the Luxury Rate higher or lower is just one way to keep your citizens happy. Other options will be explored later.

Find City

Once your civilization has begun to expand and you have built up multiple cities, you may start getting confused as to where specific cities are located on the map. Using the Find City option allows you to type in quickly the name of the city you wish to locate. The main map screen then will move to that location. Using this option allows you to keep a close eye on what's happening around you.

If several cities are located close together or a city has several units placed around it, the name of the city may be concealed on the screen. Just double-click on the concealed city and its City screen will be activated.

Options

Under the Options pull-down menu are user-selectable game play features in a submenu with several options:

- Instant Advice
- Autosave
- End of Turn
- Animations
- Sound
- Enemy Moves
- Civilopedia Text
- Palace

An option is turned on if a check mark is located next to the option. As a new player, you will definitely want to ensure that **Instant Advice** is activated.

Some versions of Civilization contain a programming error. Be sure to read the section on bugs later in this book to discover how the Instant Advice option might be affected.

The **Autosave** feature (an alternative to the manual Save Game option) will automatically save your game data every fifty turns.

While this game does not offer a lot of animated action graphics, there are a few animated sequences that take place—when you establish a new city, for example. If you wish to skip over these sequences, you can turn off **Animations**.

The activated **End of Turn** option saves you keystrokes. Everything that you do once your simulation begins is done in *turns*. Each turn represents a shift in time period of between one and twenty years, during which you will implement your strategies by moving active units. After each turn, the computer will automatically proceed (if the End of Turn option is selected).

Save Game

Since a typical simulation can last many hours, you may want to complete a game over several sittings. At any point in a simulation, you can save the game data using the Save Game feature, which will allow you to continue playing from the same point at a later time. When you select this feature, you will be asked on what disk drive you want to save your game data. The program will automatically select a file name and will save the game data in one of ten predetermined locations. To change the location, use the arrow keys on the keyboard to move the highlighted bar.

The file name and description generated by the program will include your name, the name of the country you are ruling, and the year in which the simulation was saved.

Each time you save a game to a floppy disk or hard disk, approximately 50K of disk space will be required.

Revolution

As your civilization evolves, you will have the opportunity to rule using any one of six forms of government (Despotism, Anarchy,

Monarchy, Communism, the Republic, or Democracy). Each form of government offers specific advantages and disadvantages, which you will want to take advantage of as you play. To change your form of government, select Revolution from the Game pull-down menu (ALT+G), which is found in the Main Game screen.

Retire

If, during a simulation, things look grim and you want to just quit without saving the game, select the Retire option. When you retire, your current score will be displayed, the game will end, and you will be returned to the DOS prompt.

Quit to DOS

After the game data is saved using the Save Game option, the Quit to DOS feature can be used to exit the game and return you to the DOS prompt.

Issuing Orders Using the Orders Menu

Press Alt+O or click on the Orders menu option, and you will discover a submenu that will be used frequently during the simulation. The options available to you under the Orders menu will vary, depending on what type of *unit* is currently active. (A unit is a graphic icon that depicts a citizen or group of citizens by type.) The *active unit* will be the one flashing on the map portion of the Main Game screen.

To move the active unit, use the directional arrows on your keyboard. Each unit can move a predetermined number of spaces in any direction. (If an enemy is located nearby, movement will be limited.) Only one unit may be dealt with at a time, but a turn could involve making decisions for multiple units.

In addition to movement commands, units can be given orders when they are active. Here are a few of the options that may be available to you:

No Orders (space bar)   This allows you to skip a turn and not move or convey orders to the active unit.

Fortify (f)   Ground armies can use this feature to *fortify* themselves (fortifying a unit is like adding defensive armor), which makes them 50% stronger against attacks. When a military unit is fortified, it must remain stationary. Thus, it is good to fortify military units that are guarding a city's perimeter, but not those that are being sent elsewhere.

Sentry (s)   You can take an active unit and place it on Sentry duty using this command. When a unit is assigned to Sentry duty, it will automatically board any ships that leave that city.

GoTo   This command allows army units to proceed to a specific location as fast as possible. When you're under attack, this command comes in handy.

Pillage (p)   If you choose to destroy any land improvements that have been made on a square of land—for example, irrigation or mines—you can command certain types of active units to Pillage the square they occupy.

Home City (h)   If a unit has traveled from its Home City to a distant city, it is cheaper and easier to maintain that unit if you assign it a new home in the new city. To change an active unit's Home City, use this option. If the active unit is an aircraft, it will return to the nearest friendly city.

Disband Unit (d)   A unit may become outdated or unnecessary. Instead of using your resources to maintain that unit, you can disband it.

From the Orders pull-down menu, some units—such as Settlers, Diplomats, and Caravans—will be offered additional or alternate menu options (to perform additional tasks) within this submenu. We'll go into that later.

Consulting Your Advisors with the Advisors Menu

In Civilization, you are the leader. Like any smart leader, you have several top advisors to provide you with important information as you proceed. You can get information from an advisor by pressing Alt+A, and then selecting the appropriate advisor from the resulting pull-down menu (shown in Figure 5.4), or by pressing the function key assigned to a particular advisor.

Each advisor has a specialty—acting, for example, as a military or scientific specialist, as listed here:

City Status Advisor (F1)

This Advisor provides a quick overview of each of your cities—describing its size, what type of unit, wonder, or improvement it is producing, and its available resources. You'll want to access the City Status Advisor (shown in Figure 5.5) often, especially when you have established several cities.

Figure 5.4: The Advisors pull-down menu

Figure 5.5: The City Status screen

Military Advisor (F2)

Use this Advisor to track the military force at your disposal. The Military Advisor menu selection results in a report (see Figure 5.6) that will tell the number and type of military units available and/or currently in production. This option also offers you information—such as how quickly new military units can be put into action—that can be very helpful when you're in a combat situation.

Intelligence Advisor (F3)

In order to obtain Intelligence, you must first establish Diplomats, and thus, embassies. Once you've built embassies in foreign lands, you can use the Intelligence Advisor's report to learn about your enemies and allies. For example, you will be able to determine a rival city's military strength and what resources it has available.

Attitude Advisor (F4)

The Attitude Advisor option (found, again, under the Advisors pull-down menu) allows you to keep tabs on your civilization's internal maintenance—whether your people are happy, contented, or annoyed. This is the fastest way to obtain their feedback. If you really manage to piss off your citizens—by starving them or providing inadequate resources—they won't wait for you to check in for your Attitude Advisor's report; they will be sure to inform you directly, through message windows that will appear on the game screen.

MILITARY STATUS
Empire of the Romans
Emperor <<JASON>>: 2200 BC

Militia	(1/1/1)	7 active	
Phalanx	(1/2/1)	1 active	1 in pro
Cavalry	(2/1/2)	1 active	1 in pro
Chariot	(4/1/2)		1 in production

Figure 5.6: The Military Advisor's report

Trade Advisor (F5)

Your trade advisor will keep you up-to-date on how well each of your cities is doing financially. This report tells you how tax dollars are being allocated, what scientific research is being conducted, and what luxuries you've made available to your citizens.

This report also tells you how much of your financial resources is going toward maintaining city improvements, and how many additional turns are required to reach the discovery of the next advancement your scientists are pursuing. Based on the information provided by your Trade Advisor (as shown in Figure 5.7), you can determine the productivity of each of your cities.

Science Advisor (F6)

Use your Science Advisor to track your scientific achievements and the advancements your scientists are developing. The lightbulb icons displayed in the report (as shown in Figure 5.8) indicate in a quantitative way the scientific research that has been done.

The World Command
Puts the Whole Planet in Your Hands

By pressing Alt+W, or by double-clicking the mouse on the word World (located at the top of the Main Game screen), you can gain

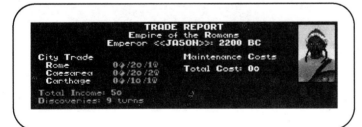

Figure 5.7: The Trade Advisor's report

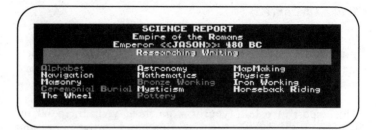

Figure 5.8: The Science Advisor's report

access to information about the entire world, not just your own civilization. This information falls into the categories:

- Wonders of the World
- Top 5 Cities
- Civilization Score
- World Map
- Demographics
- Spaceships

These options can be selected directly from the World pull-down menu (Figure 5.9) using function keys, as listed in the following section.

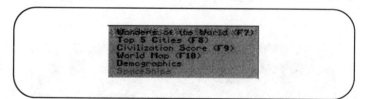

Figure 5.9: The World pull-down menu

Wonders of the World (F7)

You can use your civilization's resources to build any or all of the twenty-one Wonders of the World. Each wonder will offer your empire a specific benefit (we'll cover this in Chapter 6). Seven of these wonders are available in ancient times, seven in medieval times, and seven in modern times. Just as your civilization will try to build these wonders, so will the other civilizations on your planet. The Wonders of the World menu option will tell you where all of the existing wonders are located. (And, yes—they can be captured!)

Top 5 Cities (F8)

For a quick look at the most productive and successful cities in your world, check out this menu option—it will provide you with a basis for comparing your civilization's progress to that of the other civilizations evolving on your planet. The Top 5 Cities are determined based on score.

See Chapter 12 for details on scoring.

Civilization Score (F9)

The ultimate goal of the game is to score over 1,000 points, which will occur around the same time you explore and colonize space. The Civilization Score menu option gives you a quick peek at your score's progress thus far in the game.

World Map (F10)

When you choose this menu option, the Game screen will be replaced by a map of the entire known (explored) world, centered around your capital city.

Demographics

This detailed report, comparing your people to others, includes: the population, your approval rating, and numbers indicating the GNP and rates for Manufactured Goods, Land Area, Literacy, Disease, Pollution, Life Expectancy, Family Size, Military Service, Annual Income, and Productivity.

Spaceships

Space, "the final frontier," isn't available until the later portions of the game—your quest toward space kicks off once you have obtained the Apollo Program Wonder of the World. When you start building spaceships, chances are that other civilizations will also have this technology, so you're going to have to win the race into space. You can then use this menu option to track the status of the spaceship you have under development.

The Civilopedia: Your Guide to Being a Ruler

Think of Civilization's Civilopedia as your electronic user's guide for being a supreme leader. This fact-filled reference contains upwards of 150 tidbits pertaining to various aspects of the game. To make research fast and easy, the Civilopedia has been divided into six primary categories:

- Complete
- Civilization Advances
- City Improvements
- Military units
- Terrain Types
- Miscellaneous

Many topics listed in the Civilopedia span both a general information screen describing the topic and its relation to real-life history, and a second screen describing how the general information might be pertinent to the particular simulation.

When you press Alt+C on the keyboard, or double-click the mouse on the word Civilopedia, a submenu will appear. From this submenu you can pick a topic, such as City Improvements, and then look up a specific Improvement, such as Banks or Hydro Plants.

From the Civilopedia pull-down menu, you can get a complete listing (in alphabetical order, as shown in Figure 5.10) of all entries within the Civilopedia, or you can further narrow your search by selecting one of the general topics in the list.

Civilization Advances

This portion of the Civilopedia describes each of the technological advances available in the simulation (there are more than seventy), and describes how each advance fits into the scheme of the rest of the game.

To help you understand how each advancement is related to the next, and to the evolution and expansion of your civilization, the advances are described in detail and illustrated in charts in Chapter 9 of this book.

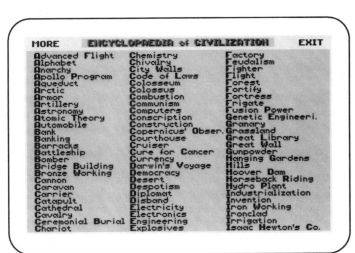

Figure 5.10: The complete Civilopedia menu list

City Improvements

Here you can gain access to information on the various City Improvements available to you, including the Wonders of the World and their advantages to your civilization. Before some City Improvements can be achieved, they require the achievement of specific technological advances—for example, the Automobile can't be built before you have invented the Wheel.

Military Units

To better understand the power and capabilities of each type of military unit, you'll want to review this area of the Civilopedia, which also covers information on Diplomats and Caravans.

See the section called "Your Civilization is Comprised of Units," in Chapter 6, for more information on military units.

Terrain Types

As we've discussed previously, many types of terrain are available on which you can build your civilization and its cities. (For a complete list of Terrain Types, see Figure 5.11.) Each type of terrain offers advantages and drawbacks. Turn to the Terrain Types portion of the Civilopedia or the "Understanding the Lay of the Land" section in Chapter 6 for more information.

Miscellaneous

The Miscellaneous subsection of the Civilopedia (Figure 5.12) contains information that just didn't fit under other headings—for example, the types of government available in the game.

The Main Game Screen Windows and Maps

A vast amount of information can be learned from the options found under the various pull-down menus; however, there is also a substantial amount of information constantly available to you on the game screens in the form of maps and windows.

Figure 5.11: The Civilopedia Terrain Types menu

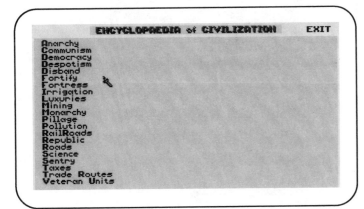

Figure 5.12: The Civilopedia Miscellaneous menu

The Unit Information Window

Along with the large map and the pull-down menus on the Main Game screen (see Figure 5.13), you'll see a Unit Information window, which will keep you informed about the population of your civilization, the current year, the funds available to you, and the Tax Rate, Luxury Rate, and Scientific Rate you have selected from the Game pull-down menu. Also featured in this area is an environmental indicator, which will be handy for helping you control pollution when that becomes an issue.

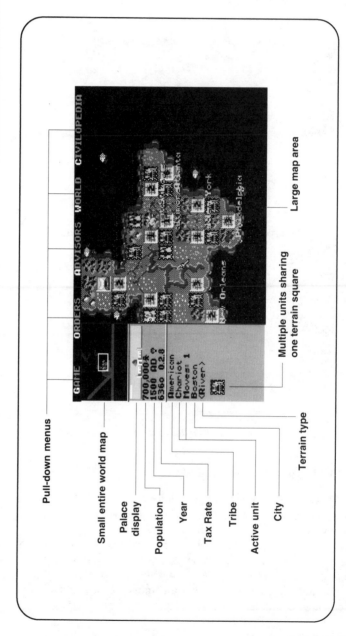

Figure 5.13: The Main Game screen at an advanced point in the game

Much of the information within the Unit Information window can and will change constantly as each turn takes place. Use this window to track how quickly your population and finances are growing or shrinking, and at what intervals time is passing.

Your Palace

Above the Unit Information window is a small graphic model of the outside of your Palace, which depicts the additions that have occurred since the start of the game.

The Small Entire World Map

In the upper-left portion of the Main Game screen, just above the picture of the Palace, is a tiny map of the entire explored world. You can double-click your mouse on any portion of this smaller world to quickly scroll around the larger map in the center of the Main Game screen and get an instant overview of known cities, oceans, and land masses, as well as of the unexplored blank areas.

Active Unit Information

The bottom-left portion of the Main Game screen displays information about the active unit. From this data, you can easily determine from what city the active unit came, what type of unit it is, how many squares in any direction it can move during a turn, what type of terrain lies beneath it, and what other units may be *under* the active unit (it is possible for units to pile up on one square of land).

If multiple units are on one terrain square, the active unit will flash, and icons representing the other units on the square will be displayed at the bottom of the Unit Information window, in the lower-left corner of the Main Game screen.

Understanding the City Screen

The second primary screen used within Civilization is the City screen, which graphically depicts just about everything you need to know about a specific city within your civilization. To access the City screen, double-click on the appropriate city icon found in the large map area of the Main Game screen. The City screen will automatically appear when a new city is founded.

Once your capital city is stable, you will want to expand your civilization by building additional cities. Each city will then have its own City screen.

What's What on the City Screen

The City screen is divided into multiple windows, as shown in Figure 5.14. You'll have to become acquainted with the meaning of each graphic icon to fully understand what's happening within the city.

A City screen will appear automatically when the city is initially founded, and then again when the city has completed the production of a unit, City Improvement, or Wonder of the World. You can also gain access to this screen at any time by double-clicking your mouse on the City icon that is located on the large map area. A City icon is a square with a number in the center of it, representing the overall strength of that city. Unless it is covered, the name of the city will appear near the square on the Main Game screen.

From the City screen, you can expect to obtain information about the city's location, population, resources, food storage, current production, and obtained improvements. You'll notice that each of these windows contains special graphic icons—for example, in the population roster in the upper-left portion of the City screen, several types of people are depicted, including happy citizens, unhappy citizens, and possibly *Taxmen*, *Scientists*, and *Entertainers* (three types of elite citizens assigned by the player to serve specific purposes in the game).

Creating Citizens and Assigning Their Roles

It is from the City screen that you have the ability to create Taxmen, Scientists, and Entertainers from existing citizens, and to order the production (or purchase) of City Improvements.

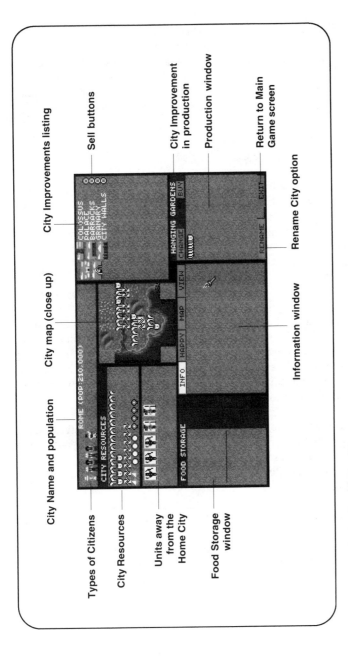

City Name and population

City map (close up)

City Improvements listing

Types of Citizens

Sell buttons

City Resources

Units away from the Home City

City Improvement in production

Production window

Food Storage window

Information window

Return to Main Game screen

Rename City option

Figure 5.14: What's what on the City screen

Located near the center of the City screen is another map of the city and its immediate surroundings. From this, the Close-up City map, you can determine the jobs your citizens are assigned to do, based on the amount of wheat (which represents farming) that is visible. You can also see the size of your population, represented both graphically and numerically, by checking the upper-left corner of the City map.

Workers and the Elite

As you will see from the graphic depiction of your citizens found in the upper-right portion of the City screen, there are two primary types of people in your population—workers and elites. The workers in your population can be happy, content, or unhappy with your leadership abilities.

To keep a city from entering a state of civil disorder, you'll want to ensure that it maintains more happy people than unhappy people.

Elite citizens (those who have been made into Taxmen, Scientists, and Entertainers) have much more power in the city, in that they help to build improvements, units, and wonders; however, creating them results in a decrease in production for that city, because to create an elite citizen means that someone had to be taken out of the workforce and converted into a new position.

Entertainers are meant to keep the population happy (or at least content). As your city grows and becomes productive, you'll want **Taxmen** to boost the city's efficiency, and to generate better tax revenues. **Scientists** can boost the creation/discovery of technological advances.

Don't create elite citizens until the city becomes productive and can maintain an adequate storage of food. Also, keep in mind that the use of Entertainers is only a quick and temporary fix for changing the attitude of the city's population.

Tracking City Improvements: The City Improvements List

Located in the upper-right portion of the City screen is the City Improvements list. As each city purchases or produces a City Improvement, the icon representing the improvement will be displayed within the City Improvements list. At the start of the game, the only item listed within the City Improvements listing will be the Palace (automatically built within your capital city when it was founded). You can use this window to quickly determine whether the overall needs of the city are being met.

Some improvements, such as Granaries, are necessary to maintain the city's growth and population, while other improvements, such as the Apollo Program Wonder of the World, are necessary to progress in the game. Maintaining a good balance between these improvements will be productive in the long run.

Maintaining City Improvements

The improvements made to each city are worth money. If you find your finances becoming seriously low, it is possible to sell a City Improvement; however, you won't want to sell something the city requires to maintain its population. For example, a Granary is important for storing surplus food to feed a growing population. If you decide to sell the city's Granary, the city *could* experience a famine shortly thereafter.

Developing and Purchasing Improvements: The Production Window

One of the most important windows within the City screen is the Production window, from which you determine which City Improvement you wish to develop or purchase. The Production window can be found on the right side of the City screen, below the City Improvements list. If you double-click your mouse on the Change button found in the Production window, you can select the City Improvement you wish to develop or purchase. Instead of waiting until you have enough resources to construct from scratch a City

Improvement or unit (once you select it from the Change menu icon), you can immediately purchase it for the listed price, if you have enough resources in your treasury.

To discover the cost of a unit, improvement, or wonder, first select the item using the Change icon, then double-click on the Buy icon (next to the Change icon) to see the item's price.

As your civilization becomes more technologically advanced, the number of different types of units and City Improvements available to you will grow. (See the Advances charts in Chapter 9 to determine the best path to take in order to achieve specific advances.) At any time during the production of a unit or City Advance (some will develop only after many turns) you can change your mind and reallocate your resources to produce a different unit or City Improvement. For example, if you receive a surprise attack from an enemy, you may want extra military units at your disposal.

There is only *one* of each Wonder of the World. If you have assigned one of your cities to develop a Wonder of the World, but find that another civilization is discovering that wonder first, you should reallocate your resources to pursue something else. Later, when you learn where that wonder is located, you can launch an attack and capture it.

Once a City Improvement is built or achieved, use the Change button to reallocate your city's resources toward working on a different improvement or Wonder of the World. Each city can build one of each City Improvement and an unlimited number of each type of unit. There is, however, only one of each wonder available to be built, so no two cities can have the same wonder.

Information on Trade Routes and Pollution: The Information Window

Near the center of the City screen is the Information window. Once the city develops trade routes with other cities, that fact will be displayed within this area, along with information about the revenue generated from the trade route.

Later in the game, when your city has the capability to create pollution and other environmental hazards, this fact will also be displayed within the Information window.

Producing and Maintaining a Surplus: The Food Storage Window

The window marked Food Storage (also on the City screen) will contain information that tells you whether the city's production capabilities can adequately feed the population, with some surplus.

An excellent strategy is to ensure that each city is producing (and can store) a surplus of food—because, as your population grows, you're going to need more food.

Tracking Remote Units: The Home City Screen

Just above the Food Storage window is the Home City screen. Here you can see instantly the various units from that city that are currently outside of the city. For example, you will see graphic icons representing the various military units protecting the city or exploring.

Remote (exploring) units are no longer inside the Home City, but the city is still supporting them. Their maintenance uses city resources, especially if the units are far from their Home City. Under the Orders pull-down menu, it is possible to reassign a unit to a new Home City, so that you can reduce the cost of maintaining that unit.

Knowing What's Available: The City Resources Window

The final window on the City screen is the City Resources window. Within this window are several different graphic icons—representing food, resources, trade, luxuries, corruption, tax revenue, trade, scientific research, surplus food, and surplus resources, and indicating how much of each of these the city is generating.

Exactly what appears within the City Resources window will depend upon what you have assigned the population to accomplish.

For example, wheat symbols represent farming and food production. Coins mean your city is geared for industrial production (manufacturing). If many lightbulbs appear in the City Resources window, it means you have created a lot of scientists.

Some City Improvements, such as Factories, have a direct impact on production. How each element within the Resources Window works within the simulation will be discussed in Chapter 8.

Chapter 6

The Elements of Civilization

This chapter continues a detailed overview of Civilization's basic elements, in particular the government types, terrain squares, military and non-military units, the City Improvements, and the Wonders of the World.

In the Government Your People Trust

The people in your civilization rely on their government for *everything*. As the leader of the government, that puts you in the hot seat. Within Civilization there are six types of governments; however, several of those are available only after you have obtained certain advances. For example, Democracy only becomes available in later parts of a simulation, after you have acquired basic knowledges, such as: Writing, Code of Laws, Literacy, Mysticism, and Philosophy. The best time to switch to a Democracy is when most of the rival empires have been defeated and you are living in peaceful and stable times.

Other forms of government are available only under certain circumstances—for example, when Anarchy appears in a time of civil disorder after an invasion.

Changing Governments

Each form of government offers its own advantages and disadvantages in terms of your civilization's growth and well-being.

Further discussion of government types will follow later in this chapter, as well as in the strategy chapters of this book.

At the start of the simulation, Despotism (defined in the next section of this chapter) is in place. By ordering a Revolution (using the Game pull-down menu) you have the ability to change the existing form of government.

As you progress in a simulation, you will find that more advanced forms of government allow your population to greatly increase production and better manage its finances. No matter what type of government exists, you're still in charge.

The Types of Government Available

The forms of government that are or will be available within the simulation include:

- Despotism
- Anarchy
- Monarchy
- Communism
- The Republic
- Democracy

Now, in case you were asleep in class when they taught about forms of government, here are brief definitions that should prove helpful:

Despotism: is a government in which the people are controlled by an absolute ruler—either a benevolent despot, or a tyrant. (That's you, when you're playing Civilization.)

Anarchy: is an absence of government. In Civilization, Anarchy occurs when civil disorder erupts. While no central government is in existence, no taxes are collected, no scientific research is conducted, and no progress is made on City Improvements.

When the time comes to change government types (in order to improve overall production and growth and to slow down corruption) you may have to go through a period of Anarchy.

Monarchy: a government led by a *monarch* (a person who reigns by "divine right" over a kingdom or an empire). This form of government gives less control to the ruler than does Despotism, but makes the population happier and more productive. In Civilization, when it comes to production, there are definite advantages to ruling your civilization as a Monarchy rather than through Despotism.

In Civilization, the happier your people are, the harder they work, the faster they reproduce, and the less you will have to do to *keep* them happy.

Communism: a system of government in which goods and production are commonly owned, although a government and its leader—you—still retain decision-making powers. Under Civilization's Communism, there is less corruption.

Building Banks and/or Courthouses also helps to control corruption.

The Republic: a political system where elected representatives exercise power over the people. When your civilization opens trade routes with other countries, you'll want to rule under The Republic, which gives the population some additional freedom.

As a ruler under the Republic, however, you'll find that the senate can override your decisions to break a treaty or invade a foreign country. And, when a foreign country approaches you to make peace, the senate will automatically accept. Under less advanced forms of government—Despotism, Monarchy, and Communism—you, as the ruler, have the option to simply reject a peace offering and to declare war.

Democracy: a form of government exercised either directly by the people through the ruling of a majority vote, or through the vote of the people's elected representatives. Democracy—the most advanced form of government in the game—makes the population happiest, and gives you the best opportunity to expand production and trade. As is true in the Republic, some of your decisions in a Democracy (i.e., whether to attack or sign a peace treaty) must be approved by the senate.

Understanding the Lay of the Land

One key to succeeding in Civilization is understanding the terrain and taking full advantage of it. Just as is true on Earth, the planet you inhabit while playing this simulation contains many types of land (continents and islands with different terrains) and water (rivers, lakes, and oceans). At the start of a game, your knowledge of the land and water is extremely limited (which is why you must *explore*).

Exploring and Exploiting Terrain Squares

In Civilization, the entire planet is broken up into *squares* (or units on a grid). Each square represents an area of land that contains a specific type of terrain—such as Grasslands, Plains, or Swamps—that you may take advantage of as you establish your cities and expand your civilization. Land can be used to provide natural resources such as food, or additional wealth in the form of gems or minerals, or it can be used to defend your cities from enemies (military units can't cross water without boats, for example). As you will soon discover, some terrain is more useful and valuable for your purposes than other terrain.

Terrain Types Make a Difference

The types of terrain found within your simulated planet can include:

Arctic Areas   These squares of frigid terrain cannot produce food or encourage trade. Thus, this type of area is far from ideal for settling your civilization.

Desert Regions   These hot, dry areas can be irrigated and become productive, but in Civilization it is best to create trade routes by building roads through Desert areas.

Hills   When you find hills, start building mines so that you can take full advantage of the natural resources available. Mining for minerals, oil, or gems is an excellent way to increase your civilization's finances. Hills can also be irrigated, which will make them suitable for habitation.

Mountains Strategically placing cities *near* mountains can give you a bit of added protection from enemies. However, building your city on a mountain is not great—most mountains have a minimal water supply, which makes feeding people difficult. Mountains are good for mining, but useless for agriculture.

Grasslands As you initially expand, Grasslands are ideal locations for building cities, because you can easily grow food nearby. To create an ideal situation, irrigate Grasslands and the city you've founded nearby will be all set in terms of food production.

Ocean To establish trade routes with other civilizations, you will probably travel across oceans. This can only be done by building boats, and later aircraft. Cities assigned to producing boats *must* be near the water.

Jungle Living in the jungle does not give you access to any great resources. However, you can expand into Jungle areas and then convert them into Grasslands or Forests that are far *more* suitable for cities.

To convert terrain, select Change To (Terrain Type) on the Orders pull-down menu. Only a Settlers unit can convert terrain squares. This must be done before a city is founded on the square.

Swamps Swampland is not the place to found your capital city, but as you expand, it can be converted into Grasslands or Forest areas.

Rivers Building cities near Rivers is an excellent strategy—growing food near a river is easy, and rivers provide a pathway for trade routes. Like Grasslands, River areas are ideal locations for founding your capital city and other early cities.

Cities near rivers must be protected or, as progress occurs, an enemy ship could sail up the river and launch an attack.

Forest   Forest areas in Civilization are adequate but not ideal for supporting cities. If you must found a city in a Forest area, you may wish to convert the land first.

Plains   This type of terrain—open and flat, allowing for agriculture—is rich in resources, but should be irrigated to maximize your internal growth and production potential.

Tundra   Little can be done with this treeless and somewhat arctic terrain, so avoid settling down in these areas.

Special Random Terrain Squares

As you explore various types of terrain, you will probably encounter special Random Terrain squares (marked by a graphic icon that looks like a group of tiny huts) containing hidden resources, extra funds, hidden knowledge or advances (in the form of ancient scrolls), or perhaps a friendly (or barbarian) tribe. Only by entering these squares (shown in Figure 6.1) can you see what they offer.

When you do discover a special square, it is wise to explore it with a military unit, just in case barbarians are hidden there and you are forced to fight.

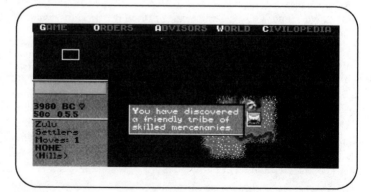

Figure 6.1: Discovering a special Random Terrain square can lead to knowledge advancements, military advancements, or a barbarian attack

Getting a Reward for Capturing Barbarians

If you capture a barbarian leader, you will be financially rewarded, but to do so, you must have the right military forces at your disposal.

If, in a special square, you discover a minor tribe that is friendly, its population may join your civilization and give you certain benefits or bonus items. For example, if the small friendly tribe has an advance, such as Horseback Riding, which your civilization has not yet acquired, that advance (knowledge) will become yours.

Other Resources Associated with Terrain Types

In addition to offering specific advantages, certain types of terrain may also contain special resources, such as:

Fish	found in the Oceans
Coal	found in the Hills
Game	animal life found in Forest and Tundra areas
Gems	stones, valuable for trading, found in Jungles
Horses	found in the Plains
Gold	discovered in Mountains
Oil	found in Swamps
Oasis	sometimes found in the Desert

Often, you can take advantage of these special resources without settling in the terrain squares that contain them.

Your Civilization Is Comprised of Units

To make it easier to manage your population, which extends out of its Home City in the form of *units* (graphic representations of citizens or military) that move around the game screen, Civilization divides your people into different *types* of individual units, each of which has its own responsibilities and capabilities.

Each unit occupies one square on the large game play map. During each turn, one unit at a time will become the *active* unit, which means you have control over it and must issue it orders or tell it where to move.

During a turn, you can select non-active units and make them active by double-clicking on them (individually) with your mouse.

Depending on the type of unit, it will move a predetermined number of squares (or spaces) around the map. You determine in what direction a unit will move, unless the GoTo option (found under the Orders pull-down menu on the Main Game screen) is selected.

As a rule, building and using Roads and Railroads enables many units to travel greater distances each time they become active.

You can choose to keep an active unit stationary (in its present square) while you move other units, and then return to move the first unit. To do this, press W (for Wait) on the keyboard. If you do not wish to return to the active unit during the current turn, press the space bar.

It is also possible for multiple units—for example, two Chariot units—to share one square on the map. Some units are even designed to *require* that other units share their space—a ship or an aircraft, for example, carries other units (such as Caravans, Diplomats, and military units) via the oceans or rivers to other land masses and continents. If you are being invaded by an enemy, you could lose all of the units located on a single square during the attack.

If a unit is fortified, it will remain in one location during a turn, and won't become active automatically. As a fortified unit, however, its defensive strength increases by 50%. Thus, it is wise to fortify a unit that is defending a city. Conversely, a fortified unit cannot launch an attack.

The Non-Military Types of Units

The following is a roundup of the types of units that you will be able to create and manage during a game. As your civilization expands, you could easily create dozens, perhaps hundreds of different units. While there is no limit to the number of each type of unit you can create, you'll want to develop a well-rounded civilization (comprised of different type of military units, along with Caravans, Settlers, and Diplomats) that is also protected with the best, most advanced military units currently available.

To conserve resources and funds, be sure to dissolve any unneeded or outdated units as your civilization expands and evolves.

Settlers   At the very start of Civilization, your population consists of a small group of nomadic Settlers, who form the population of your capital (first) city. In order for the civilization to expand after the first city is formed, you must create additional groups of Settlers. This is done by selecting Settlers from the Production window on the City screen (as shown in Figure 6.2).

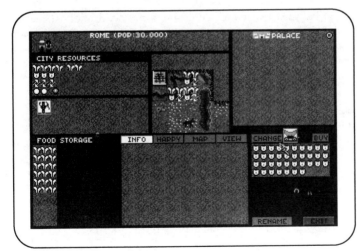

Figure 6.2: Create new Settlers in the City screen

In addition to founding cities, Settlers build Irrigation systems, Fortresses, Roads, Railroads, and Mines for their Home City; and they later clean up Polluted areas, one square at a time.

Diplomats When it comes to foreign affairs (both in times of peace and war), having Diplomats can provide you with vast information about foreign countries. Diplomats can open trade routes or act as ambassadors, saboteurs, or special intelligence agents, depending on the current situation and the decisions that you make for them. When you explore other lands and foreign cities, if the resources are available to you, it's an excellent idea to send along a Diplomat.

These guys can travel on most types of boats or planes. You will find that Diplomats and Caravans (for trading) can enter foreign cities easily, without attacking the foreign cities first.

Caravans When you're ready to establish trade routes with foreign countries and other friendly cities, you must create Caravans to transport goods or supplies to be traded or sold.

Trade between two cities within the same civilization (domestic trade) is also possible if the two cities are located a good distance apart. When a new trade route is established between foreign or domestic cities, the city that initiated the trade route will instantly reap the financial rewards, and receive ongoing financial benefits.

The Military Units: Protect and Expand Your Empire

At the core of every civilization you create within this simulation must be a strong (but not necessarily a large) military, which can protect your cities and help you expand. Of course, the power of your military will be tested should your civilization enter a war.

Militia and Phalanx Units: Your First Defense

At the early part of the game, the most powerful (and the *only*) military unit available to each city is an ordinary Militia. Later,

Phalanx units become available, and still later, other types. For now, let's talk about the earlier stages of your military.

Militia   A Militia unit is generally made up of a small portion of your population that is armed with relatively small weapons. A Militia unit can move one space per turn. When you assign a city to create Militia units, a new unit can be created every ten turns. A Militia unit can be fortified to provide a city with a bit of extra protection, but that fortified unit cannot move unless it is unfortified and activated.

When you first establish a city early in the game, you'll want to protect it with at least two or three Militia units that are fortified. Units produced later can then explore, expanding your civilization.

Just about any military unit can be fortified, using the Fortify command from the Orders pull-down menu.

Ideally, you'll want to upgrade your military by creating more powerful military units as soon as possible, and by disbanding outdated units to conserve resources and finances.

As a general rule, the more powerful the military unit, the more resources it will take to create or purchase. While you may wish to create a large number of military units, you should consider whether or not you would be better served by a smaller number of stronger (more powerful) units.

Phalanx   After Militia units, the next step up on the military scale is Phalanx units, which are a bit stronger from a defensive standpoint. Phalanx units can also move just one space per turn; however, it takes twenty turns, rather than ten, to create a Phalanx unit. Additionally, your civilization must have obtained the Bronze Working advance before the first Phalanx unit can be created.

After one or two Phalanx units have been created, fortify them and have them replace the Militia units currently protecting your city (or cities). Then, because the city is better protected, you can reactivate the Militia units (that were fortified) and use them for exploration, or you can disband the Militia units if you have alternate units that can be used for exploration.

Building Military Strength

In later stages of the game, when a new city is being created close to an established, well-protected one, you can immediately assign the new city to create more powerful military or non-military units (which take additional turns and greater resources to create). If two cities are founded too close together, however, they could abuse the nearby resources, which could lead to problems with food production, etc.

In addition to Militia and Phalanx units, over twenty other types of military units are (or will be) available as the simulation progresses. To be successful in managing and expanding your civilization, you will not necessarily have to use every one of these military units. By the middle stages of the simulation, the types of units you will require will depend on circumstances such as the decisions you make and the objectives you set.

Along with military units, an excellent way to protect a city is to build City Walls, especially for cities located near the water. Barbarians can attack cities by approaching them from the water. City Walls offer much better protection than basic fortification.

The More Powerful Military Units

Along with Militia and Phalanx units, you can create numerous other types of military units (listed alphabetically and described below). To determine what military units you have built or are building, consult your Military Advisor (Figure 6.3) by pressing Alt+A (or F2) and selecting the Military Advisor option. For additional information about each type of military unit, see the charts in Chapter 9.

Armor When it comes to extra maneuverability (up to three spaces during each turn), Armor units (tank forces) are excellent for launching ground-based attacks. (The Automobile advancement is required.)

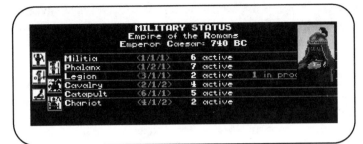

Figure 6.3: The Military Advisor will report on how many of each type of military unit is available to your empire

Artillery   Because it has a good offensive and defensive rating in the game, this military unit provides vast power, but takes a lot of resources to manufacture. If a foreign city is protected by City Walls, use Artillery to shoot over the walls. (The Robotic advancement is required.)

Battleship   Ideal for defeating other ships or shooting from water to land, these units have an extremely strong defense rating, but can't carry or transport other units. (The Steel advancement is required.)

If you discover that your initial cities are located on an island, you will want to follow a development plan that will allow you to build ships early on. Ships can only be launched if they are built by a city located near water. To increase the power of your navy, build a Lighthouse.

Bomber   These aircraft have limited range (in that they can't move too many squares in a turn), but can be used for launching powerful air-based attacks. Bombers won't be available to you until the later stages of the game. (The Advanced Flight advancement is required.)

Cannon   In the middle stages of the simulation, after the Metallurgy advancement is obtained, Cannon units can be used for launching powerful land-based attacks.

Carrier   Once you have obtained the Advanced Flight advancement, you're on your way to building a powerful air force. A Carrier is a water-based unit that can be used as a mobile base for Bombers, Fighters, and other aircraft.

Catapult   If you chose to pursue the Mathematics advancement in the early stages of the simulation, your city or cities will have the capability to build Catapults, which are excellent for defensive and offensive military maneuvers. These units have a high offensive rating and are relatively inexpensive (in terms of resources) to build, yet they will prove extremely valuable when it comes to battle against rival civilizations or barbarians.

Cavalry   The major advantage to launching a horseback Cavalry unit is its ability to travel quickly. (As you may have guessed, the Horseback Riding advancement is required.)

Chariot   Upon discovering the Wheel (an advancement you should acquire early on) you will discover that Chariots are great for launching attacks, for defense, and for exploration.

Cruiser   Like the Battleship, the Cruiser is a powerful ship that can travel great distances (up to six spaces) during a single turn. (The Combustion advancement is required.)

Fighter   This unit, representing fighter planes, must return to a base after each turn, but it can move ten spaces during a turn. In the early stages of flight, Fighters are a powerful resource for establishing an air force. (The Flight advancement is required.)

Frigate   For fairly early sea exploration (or travel over water to reach other lands), a Frigate unit can move quickly and carry other military or non-military units. (The Magnetism advancement is required.)

On ships that can carry other units, try to place at lease one ground-based unit that can be used to explore new land masses that you discover. Based on what you find, you can later transport additional military units, Caravans, or Diplomats.

Ironclad If you're forced to enter into ship-to-ship battles, Ironclads will give you a powerful advantage. These ships can move up to four squares per move. (The Steam Engine advancement is required.)

Knights In the earlier stages of your civilization's development, while still in ancient and medieval times, Knights can be used for offense and defense (after the Chivalry advancement is obtained).

Legion After you have obtained the Iron Working advancement, creating Legions (groups of armed soldiers) offers a cheap, fast method of building up your ground-based army. Legion units offer decent defense strength, but can move only one square per turn.

Mechanized Infantry In terms of ground forces, you can't beat a Mechanized Infantry unit for offensive and defensive strength. They can travel up to three spaces per turn, but require a significant amount of resources to build. (The Labor Union advancement is required.)

Musketeers Upon the discovery of Gunpowder, Musketeers outdate and can replace Militia and Phalanx units that are being used to defend cities and other areas. Musketeers, because they are armed with guns, offer better offensive and defensive strengths than Militia or Phalanx units.

Nuclear The ultimate offensive attack capability, the use of Nuclear weapons, gives you extreme power. Nuclear missiles, which are transportable, can be built only after Rocketry and Nuclear Fission have been discovered and the Manhattan Project Wonder of the World has been built by a civilization.

Riflemen Because rifles are more accurate and advanced than muskets, this type of military unit is the next step up from Musketeers in terms of ground forces. (The Conscription advancement is required.)

Sail The first reliable type of naval ship available to you will probably be the basic sailing ship. (The less reliable Frigates sink if they get too far from land.) This Sail unit can be used for exploring uncharted waters or for transporting a limited number of units (per trip) to other land masses. (The Navigation advancement is required.)

Submarine For advanced ship-to-ship battles, Submarines offer special advantages: it is hard for enemy ships to detect them, and submarines have strong offensive and defensive ratings. Submarines cannot transport other units. (The Mass Production advancement is required.)

Transport When you are ready to plan an all-out attack on a foreign country located across water, a Transport unit can be used to carry up to eight other units. This type of ship can travel four spaces per turn. (The Industrialization advancement is required.)

Trireme These small ships are totally unreliable, because they often get lost at sea if they travel too far from land. They are good for exploring coastline or transporting units very short distances over water. Do not use these ships to transport key units over great distances—if a Trireme becomes lost, whatever other units it was carrying are also lost. (The Map Making advancement is required.)

City Improvements

At any given time, a city's resources can be used to create one new unit, or a City Improvement. City Improvements can be used to enhance productivity, or to better manage a city by offering the citizens a luxury. While City Improvements can take many turns and a lot of resources to build, each offers a benefit to its Home City and/ or to your civilization as a whole.

Each city can build only one of each type of improvement. Once built, a City Improvement can be lost to sabotage, disaster, or capture. To raise funds quickly, a City Improvement can also be sold.

To sell an Improvement, access the City screen and double-click on the Sell button found in the City Improvements listing.

After building (or purchasing) a City Improvement, there is a predetermined fee charged, per turn, for managing it. If the city can't afford these ongoing fees, the improvement will automatically be sold.

If your funds begin to run extremely low and a particular city can't afford to maintain its City Improvements, the computer will automatically select an improvement in that city to sell. Thus, to control which City Improvement gets sold when times are rough, decide in advance which less-needed improvements you are willing to sell—do this *before* funds get low and the computer (acting on behalf of your citizens) reacts.

Early in the game, the first City Improvement you will have the opportunity to build is military-related Barracks. Barracks require no extra knowledge or advancements to build, and they are pretty cheap, because they require no maintenance fees. Once built, they increase the strength of that city's ground-based military units by 50%. In addition to Barracks, you have the option to allocate a city's resources to build any one of twenty other City Improvements or twenty-one different Wonders of the World.

Aqueduct   Not only will building an Aqueduct protect a city from randomly occurring disasters such as Fire and Plagues, but it will also enhance irrigation and thus production, allowing the city population to expand. *Cost*: 120 resources, plus $2.00 per turn to maintain.

Bank   In Civilization, a Bank increases the effective use of taxes and luxuries by 50%, while helping to stop corruption in the city. Before building a Bank, your city must first contain a Marketplace. *Cost*: 120 resources, plus $3.00 per turn to maintain.

Barracks   Barracks increase the attack and defense strength of early ground-based military units by 50%, while eliminating the threat of pirates (another "natural" disaster). There is no maintenance cost per turn to maintain Barracks. It is a wise move to build Barracks in each of your cities early in their development. You can later sell this improvement just before your civilization discovers Gunpowder and Combustion, since these advances cause Barracks to become outdated. *Cost*: 20 resources; no maintenance.

Cathedral Once you have established Religion within a city, building a Cathedral is an excellent way to keep the population happy. *Cost*: 160 resources, plus $3.00 per turn to maintain.

City Walls In addition to protecting the city from Floods (natural disasters) building City Walls will triple that city's defense capabilities. This Improvement is ideal for protecting large, well-established cities that contain resources you especially would not want to lose as a result of an attack. To build City Walls, you must first learn Masonry. *Cost*: 120 resources, plus $2.00 per turn to maintain. (An excellent investment.)

Colosseum Building a Colosseum will make a limited number of citizens happy. Because of its high building cost, a Colosseum is not the ideal improvement to consider—other improvements are cheaper and provide similar results. *Cost*: 100 resources, plus $4.00 per turn to maintain.

Courthouse After you have developed a Code of Laws, you can reduce corruption by 50% simply by building a Courthouse, which represents an organized legal system with judges and police. *Cost*: 80 resources, plus $1.00 per turn to maintain. (Definitely a wise investment for cities that are more likely to experience more corruption beccause of larger populations and established trade routes.)

Factory By building a Factory, you can increase the resources produced within that city by 50%. A regular Factory becomes obsolete when a Manufacturing Plant is built. *Cost*: 200 resources, plus $4.00 per turn to maintain.

Granary Every growing city should invest in a Granary (a building in which food is stored) as its population begins to increase. A Granary helps a city to manage its food supply and to prevent Famine. Since you'll want to build a Granary in your capital city early in the game, develop Pottery (a prerequisite) as soon as possible. *Cost*: 60 resources, plus $1.00 per turn to maintain.

Hydro Plant Not only will a Hydro Plant (a water-based energy source) allow the Factories and Manufacturing Plants in your cities to increase production, but it will also help to avoid pollution. You must first develop Electronics, then you'll be able to build a Hydro Plant. *Cost*: 240 resources, plus $4.00 per turn to maintain.

Library   If you're looking to increase the speed of scientific advancements, building a Library will help. You'll need to develop Writing first. *Cost*: 80 resources, plus $1.00 per turn to maintain.

Manufacturing Plant   In later stages of the civilization, once you have acquired Robotics, you can build a Manufacturing Plant to increase resources created within a city by 100%. After a Manufacturing Plant is built, add a Hydro Plant to further increase productivity. *Cost*: 320 resources, plus $6.00 per turn to maintain.

Marketplace   Once your civilization has established Currency, you can build a Marketplace to boost tax revenue and luxuries by 50% (a definite advantage early in the game). *Cost*: 80 resources, plus $1.00 per turn to maintain.

Mass Transit   In later stages of the simulation, building a Mass Transit system will help a city to control pollution. *Cost*: 160 resources, plus $4.00 per turn to maintain.

Nuclear Power Plant   Use a Nuclear Power Plant to increase production of Factories and Manufacturing Plants by 50% while controlling pollution within the city. The drawback to a Nuclear Power Plant is the possibility of a nuclear meltdown if the people of the city become aggravated and civil disorder occurs. *Cost*: 160 resources, plus $4.00 per turn to maintain.

Palace   When your capital city is founded, so is your Palace. As your civilization expands, however, and cities are built at great distances from the Palace, corruption may take place. If a Palace is destroyed or needs to be moved (so as to better manage the entire civilization), there is a rebuilding cost of 200 resources. If you are a good leader, your population will automatically decide to build extensions to your Palace. There are *no costs* for the Palace or its extensions.

Power Plant   Instead of a Nuclear Power Plant or Hydro Plant, a Power Plant can be built. The problem with Power Plants is that they cause pollution. They do, however, increase the productivity of Factories and Manufacturing Plants by 50%. *Cost*: 160 resources, plus $4.00 per turn to maintain

Recycling Center When pollution becomes a problem within a city (and once the civilization has acquired the knowledge of recycling), building a Recycling Center can reduce pollution by $2/3$. Recycling Centers make excellent investments in later stages of the game. *Cost*: 200 resources, plus $2.00 per turn to maintain.

SDI (Strategic Defense Initiative) Defense The real-life American public refers to this type of anti-nuclear weapon system as "Star Wars." It is an important City Improvement late in the game, once the nuclear race begins. *Cost*: 200 resources, plus $4.00 per turn to maintain.

Temple Building a Temple in Civilization will help to keep the population happy, while protecting against the danger of Volcanoes (a natural disaster). *Cost*: 40 resources, plus $1.00 per turn to maintain.

University Once you've built a Library and you're looking to further expand the knowledge of your people, you can build a University to increase knowledge by 50%. Before you build a University (City Improvement), the University (scientific knowledge) advancement must be acquired, so you'll know *how* to build the University. *Cost*: 160 resources, plus $3.00 per turn to maintain.

Wonders of the World: An Overview

When we look back in history, we view many accomplishments with awe. For example, the Great Pyramid was a massive project that employed what were then state-of-the-art building skills. Your civilization has the opportunity to build many great simulated Wonders of the World, each of which offers a major benefit to your society. In order to build each of the wonders, your civilization must first have acquired the necessary knowledge and skills (of advancements and improvements). Only then can the building process begin.

When you build each wonder, your empire will receive a new knowledge or capability. These were designed by the game's developers, and may seem somewhat arbitrary.

From a scoring standpoint, each Wonder of the World is worth a different number of points. See Chapter 12 for more on scoring.

When a city is in the process of building a Wonder of the World, other cities within your civilization can lend their support by sending Caravans (which speed up the process) into the city building the wonder. When a Caravan moves into a city building a wonder, you must accept the "Help Build Wonder" option to receive the Caravan's assistance. Since it takes many turns to build a wonder, you are investing in a city's future when you assign it to build a wonder.

As you will see, there are three sets of wonders. During each of the three eras (ancient, medieval, and modern), only seven of the twenty-one Wonders of the World can be built. If another civilization has beaten you to the building of a specific wonder, you can launch a full-scale attack, capture the wonder, and receive its benefits. Once built, some wonders can provide powerful additional defenses to a city. Other wonders are ideal for improving the morale and productivity of your population.

If you're trying to please your people, build Temples, Colosseums, and Cathedrals. To improve science and knowledge, building Libraries and Universities is an excellent investment.

Wonders of the World: Ancient Era

Colossus Building this giant statue (once you have acquired Bronze Working knowledge) will increase trade revenue, and will continue to benefit the city with increased trade revenue until Electricity is created. *Cost*: 200 resources.

Great Library Before your civilization develops a University, you can build a Great Library, which will allow you to obtain any two advancements possessed by another civilization. *Cost*: 300 resources.

Great Wall
Until Gunpowder is discovered, building a Great Wall ensures that all foreign civilizations will offer you the option for peace. Thus, this City Improvement is ideal (once you have obtained the knowledge of Masonry) for civilizations looking to expand peacefully. *Cost*: 300 resources.

Hanging Gardens Once you have established Pottery, building a Hanging Garden will help to keep your population happy. Its effects, however, will stop once the knowledge of Invention is established. *Cost*: 300 resources.

Lighthouse If your civilization must take to the sea to expand or establish trade routes, building a Lighthouse (Figure 6.4) is an absolute must! This City Improvement allows ships to move faster and farther during each turn (see Figure 6.5). The knowledge of Map Making is necessary to build a Lighthouse (which will remain operational until Magnetism is discovered). *Cost*: 200 resources.

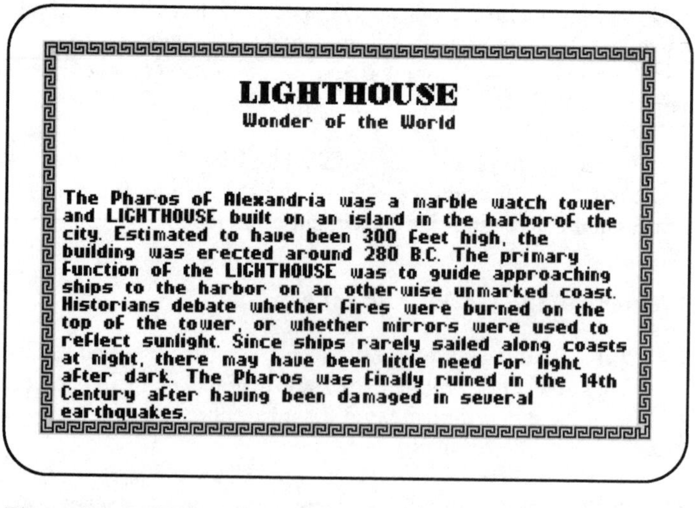

LIGHTHOUSE
Wonder of the World

The Pharos of Alexandria was a marble watch tower and LIGHTHOUSE built on an island in the harbor of the city. Estimated to have been 300 feet high, the building was erected around 280 B.C. The primary function of the LIGHTHOUSE was to guide approaching ships to the harbor on an otherwise unmarked coast. Historians debate whether fires were burned on the top of the tower, or whether mirrors were used to reflect sunlight. Since ships rarely sailed along coasts at night, there may have been little need for light after dark. The Pharos was finally ruined in the 14th Century after having been damaged in several earthquakes.

Figure 6.4: Building the Lighthouse Wonder of the World

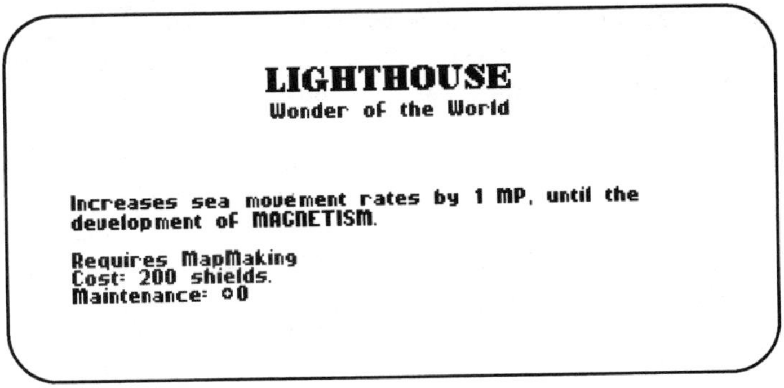

```
╭─────────────────────────────────────────────────╮
│                                                   │
│                  LIGHTHOUSE                       │
│               Wonder of the World                 │
│                                                   │
│                                                   │
│   Increases sea movement rates by 1 MP, until the │
│   development of MAGNETISM.                        │
│                                                   │
│   Requires MapMaking                              │
│   Cost: 200 shields.                              │
│   Maintenance: 0 0                                │
│                                                   │
╰─────────────────────────────────────────────────╯
```

Figure 6.5: The Lighthouse Wonder of the World information screen explains what this wonder offers your empire and the cost of maintaining it

Oracle Before formal Religion is established, an Oracle can be used to keep the population happy (once Mysticism is acquired). *Cost*: 300 resources.

Pyramids After developing Masonry skills, a city can build a Pyramid, which allows the civilization to change to any type of government (even if the civilization does not have the necessary technological advancements). A Pyramid can also keep your government from entering a state of Anarchy. *Cost*: 300 resources.

Wonders of the World: Entering the Medieval Age

As you enter a more modern era and your scientists acquire additional knowledge, they will have the opportunity to build the following Wonders of the World, which are more advanced than those that were previously available.

Copernicus's Observatory If your civilization is in pursuit of knowledge, building this wonder will double a city's knowledge production. An excellent strategy is first to build a Library and/or University, and/or to allocate extra Scientists, and *then* (after you have discovered Astronomy) to build this observatory. *Cost*: 300 resources.

Darwin's Voyage   Obtaining this wonder allows your civilization to take over any two advancements instantly; however, you must first have obtained the Railroads advancement. *Cost*: 300 resources.

Isaac Newton's College   When used in conjunction with existing Libraries and Universities, Isaac Newton's College will increase your civilization's knowledge. Before construction begins on this wonder, you must first have obtained the Theory of Gravity. The effect of this wonder (increased knowledge—or more specifically, the ability of your scientists to work harder with greater results) continues until the development of Nuclear Fission. *Cost*: 400 resources.

J.S. Bach's Cathedral   Upon establishing Religion, building this cathedral is an excellent way for keeping the population of your entire civilization happy. *Cost*: 400 resources.

Magellan's Expedition   Civilizations that have begun to explore the seas will find that Magellan's Expedition offers boats and ships the ability to travel an additional square per turn. Before acquiring this wonder, you must have developed Navigation. *Cost*: 400 resources.

Michelangelo's Chapel   After Religion is established, Michelangelo's Chapel will help keep your population happy. *Cost*: 300 resources.

To really take advantage of this wonder, first build Cathedrals—it is possible to obtain Michelangelo's Chapel *before* you have built Cathedrals, however, in combination with Cathedrals, this wonder will keep more people happy.

Shakespeare's Theatre   After obtaining the knowledge of Medicine, you can ensure that your population will remain happy (and entertained) once Shakespeare's Theatre is built. The effects of this wonder on the population's happiness will continue until Electronics is invented. *Cost*: 400 resources.

Wonders of the World: Modern Times

Apollo Program   In the later stages of a simulation, when your population is ready to trek into space, you must obtain the Apollo

Program so you can build spaceships. If your goal is to colonize space (as opposed to conquering the world), you simply must obtain this wonder. Because this wonder is symbolic of having a satellite, which would give you a broad overhead view of the explored and unexplored areas of the planet, the Apollo Program also gives you the ability to see the location of each city in the world on the small entire world map on the Main Game screen. *Cost*: 600 resources.

Cure for Cancer As your civilization advances into the future, you can invent the Cure for Cancer, which will also help to keep your population happy. *Cost*: 600 resources.

Hoover Dam This wonder benefits all of the cities on a continent by supplying power without causing pollution. Additionally, Hoover Dam increases resources generated by the city by 50%. *Cost*: 600 resources.

Manhattan Project After you obtain the knowledge of Nuclear Fission, you have access to the Manhattan Project, which allows your civilization to create nuclear weapons. However, once one city obtains this knowledge, it is available to all civilizations, including your enemies. Thus, a nuclear race could begin. *Cost*: 600 resources.

SETI Program This wonder (which is based on NASA's search for alien life) increases knowledge generated in a city by 50%, but can't be used until Computers are discovered. *Cost*: 600 resources.

When you obtain the SETI Program, you will want to have plenty of scientists to take advantage of what this wonder offers them.

Women's Suffrage Obtaining Women's Suffrage is another way to help keep your population happy, once you have discovered Industrialization. This wonder works only if your civilization is governed as a Republic or Democracy. *Cost*: 600 resources.

You can obtain a wonder (such as Women's Suffrage) at any time in the age in which it exists. However, if you lack some prerequisite for using it (such as the Republic or Democratic government types needed for Women's Suffrage), why spend the resources to obtain it?

United Nations After the advance of Communism, you can begin developing the United Nations. This wonder always gives you the opportunity to enter into a peace treaty with foreign countries you encounter. If you are currently involved in a war when this wonder is achieved, you will have the opportunity to enter peace negotiations. In the later stages of the simulation, you'll want to avoid war so that you can concentrate your efforts on scientific research and on reaching space. *Cost*: 600 resources.

Defining a Turn

You might want to think of Civilization as an ultra-glorified game of chess. Just as in chess, each player takes a *turn*—in this case, it's you against the computer. When you take your turn in a chess match, you must plan a strategy that you hope will achieve your long- and short-term goals.

The problem is, you don't know how your opponent will react, so you must also anticipate his or her actions while you plan your own strategies. Instead of moving chess pieces around a square board, in Civilization you move units around the computer-generated planet made up of squares. This aspect of the game is done in turns.

As you already know, your goal is to expertly manage and expand your civilization over time, helping it to evolve. In this game, a turn represents the passing of a period of time (twenty years, early in the game; as little as one year, later in the game). During each turn, you are given the opportunity to make decisions and to take action by manipulating the various units and altering the internal actions of each city as necessary.

When you have manipulated each of the active units (and made other decisions that may be required), the turn ends. At this point, the computer reacts to your decisions and determines the result(s) of your actions on your civilization, as well as how the other civilizations in your world will respond. After the computer has made its calculations, your next turn will begin. (Notice that time has passed.) In between your turns, other civilizations that are controlled by the computer will make their moves.

As each new turn begins, you must determine if your civilization has experienced growth and fix any weak areas in order to maintain a happy and stable society.

At the beginning of a new turn, you may encounter a natural disaster, such as a flash Flood or widespread Fire. Unless your civilization has the technology to counteract these random natural occurrences, damage or destruction may take place.

The natural (and random) disasters in Civilization include: Earthquakes, Volcanic Eruptions, Floods, Famine, Fire, Piracy, and Plagues. Certain City Improvements and Wonders of the World will help you defend against these disasters.

Civilization in a Nutshell

As you have probably deduced, Civilization is a highly complex simulation that will require you to plan ahead and to make critical decisions that will have both long-term and short-term results. Now that you are at least somewhat familiar with many of the options and commands available to you, and you can decipher what the various graphic icons on the game screens represent, you're in a good position to start experiencing what this game has to offer.

The following chapters include general and specific strategies and tips for creating and managing a successful civilization, along with valuable charts for planning strategies based on available City Improvements and achievements. A later chapter even describes methods for *cheating* in Civilization.

After reading this initial introduction to Civilization, if you're still a bit overwhelmed or confused, don't worry. Once you sit down to play, many aspects of the game will become obvious, with the use of just a little common sense.

Chapter 7

A Beginner's Tutorial

In previous chapters, you have seen specific Civilization game screens and graphic icons—the basics. This chapter, "A Beginner's Tutorial," will provide first-time players with an introduction to founding a civilization that will grow.

No two simulations are ever identical, so don't try to duplicate the moves selected in this tutorial—just think of it as an example. In the chapter that follows, we'll cover some specific game play strategies.

Events take place during this tutorial in the order that occurred during *this specific simulation*. During your simulations, these and other events may take place at different times, in different ways, and could have different results.

Starting the Game

At the C:\MPS prompt, type **CIV**. The game's credits will begin to appear on the screen. Press the space bar and a picture of the galaxy should appear (see Figure 7.1) along with the text, "In the beginning...."

Once Civilization is running, select Start a New Game from the main menu, followed by the Chieftain option from the Level Select menu.

You can skip most of the opening credits and the story and start right in playing a new game by pressing N (to select Start a New Game).

Making Pre-Game Choices

You'll be asked to choose a Level of Competition. Select 3 Civilizations (the bottom menu option). This means that there will be three opponent civilizations in your simulation.

A subsequent menu will appear, and you'll be asked to select the tribe you wish to rule. (If you'd chosen more opponent civilizations,

Figure 7.1: The game begins

you'd have a larger selection of tribes to rule.) This tutorial simulation follows the progress of the Zulu tribe and the default Leader Name selection of Shaka.

Following the completion of these pre-game choices, an information screen (like the one in Figure 7.2) will announce that in this case Shaka "has risen to become leader of the Zulus," and that the

Figure 7.2: This screen shows what knowledge your tribe already has acquired at the start of the game

tribe already has acquired basic knowledge, which will be listed. This knowledge won't be much, but it will provide the foundation upon which you, the Leader of the Zulu empire, must build.

The computer creates your planet, and a Main Game screen will appear. As you can see in Figure 7.3, every major portion of the screen will be labeled. Take a moment to become familiar with the general layout of this game screen if you have not already done so.

The Ancient Era: 4000 BC

Look at the left portion of the game screen and notice that the year is 4000 BC. Below that date you'll see an indication of the amount of funds in the tribe's treasury and some information about the Tax Rate and Luxury Rate (at the start of each simulation, these rates will be set to their default values).

Below that, you can see that the active unit is from the Zulu tribe and consists of a group of Settlers that will begin the simulation in a Plains terrain square. Press Enter and you will find your small tribe

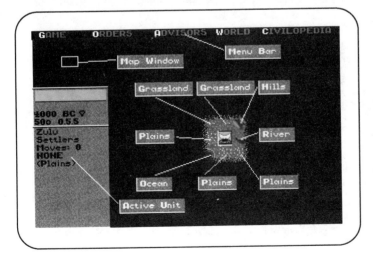

Figure 7.3: At the start of a simulation, the Main Game screen's components will be labeled

of Settlers in the center of the screen. All of the land is unexplored, so you will see blackness everywhere in both the large and small maps. Since the Chieftain option was selected, help will be offered in the form of an Information window that will state your immediate goal: to locate a suitable location to found your capital city (see Figure 7.4).

Your First Turn

Your first turn is about to begin. Press the upper-right diagonal directional key on the keyboard (usually the 9 key on the numeric keypad), and you will discover a random terrain square, as shown in Figure 7.5. This random terrain square represents a small village (notice the *hut* in the icon).

Exploring and Meeting Another Tribe

Move your settlers to the square containing this icon, and you will discover just what the icon offers—which might be knowledge or military forces you can use, or a group of barbarians that will attack you. You also will have explored a small portion of the land around you.

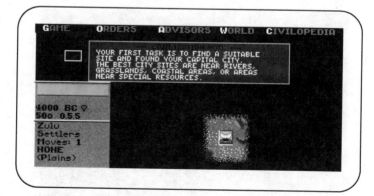

Figure 7.4: Your immediate goal is to find a suitable location for your first city

Figure 7.5: Exploring this random terrain square reveals that you have discovered a group of skilled mercenaries who will merge with your tribe

In this case, the Zulu tribe has discovered a small, friendly tribe that wants to merge and share knowledge. By merging, the Zulu tribe has just taken its first step toward growth and has obtained one Cavalry military unit in the process.

Normally, your tribe—the Zulus, in this case—would have had to obtain the knowledge of Horseback Riding to build a Cavalry unit, but when your tribe merged with the tribe found in the random terrain square, you acquired the knowledge and resources of the smaller tribe. Now, as the Zulu Settlers spend the next several turns searching for a perfect location to found the capital city, they have a bit of military protection. Notice that you now control one Cavalry unit (shown in Figure 7.6).

It's not usually a good idea to spend too many turns exploring with Settlers, but because in this case only three other civilizations exist on the planet, the chance of running into one of them is smaller.

Once again, because the Chieftain level was selected, information windows will appear periodically (like the one in Figure 7.7). In this case, the window recommends the Settler's current location (on a Plains terrain square) as an ideal place to establish a city.

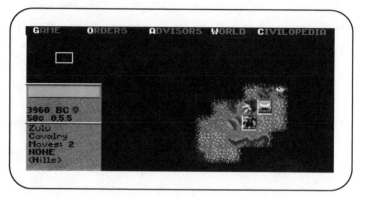

Figure 7.6: The skilled mercenaries provide the Zulu tribe with one Cavalry unit

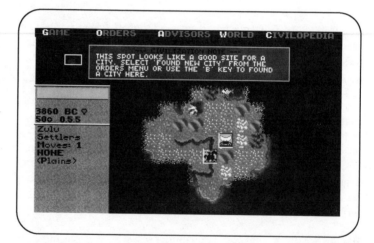

Figure 7.7: Finding an ideal location is the first step toward founding a city using a Settlers unit

Founding a Capital City

To found the capital city (or any city) when the active unit is a Settlers unit, select the Found New City option located under the Orders menu (Figure 7.8). Press Alt+O to access this menu. Since

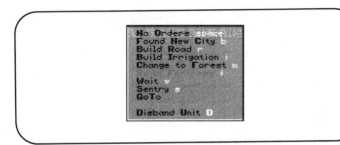

Figure 7.8: Use the Orders pull-down menu to select the Found New City option

the local territory seems somewhat safe for the moment, before founding the city, irrigate the lands by selecting the Build Irrigation option from the Orders menu. Building irrigation enhances a city's ability to grow food and maintain its population.

Now that the Settlers' terrain square has been irrigated, select the Found New City command. A default name for the new city will appear; however, you are free to type in your own city name (see Figure 7.9). In this case, the Zulu's capital city will be called Zimbabwe. Notice that the year is now 3760 BC and that several turns have passed as the Settlers continued to look for the right location to found this city.

As a city is founded, an animated graphic sequence will show the settlers moving into the area, which was barren land until now.

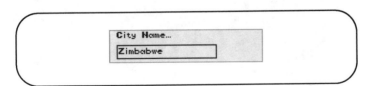

Figure 7.9: You can make up your own city name or use the default name

(Figure 7.10 depicts this sequence.) Each time a city improvement is built, you will see another animation sequence, which will show the city's growth.

Assigning the New City to Build Improvements

The City screen for Zimbabwe will appear following the animation sequence. From the City screen, you can assign City Improvements you want the capital city to develop. You can also see from the City screen that the initial population of the city is 10,000, and that the Palace for the empire has been built (see the City Improvement window in the upper-right portion of the City screen).

With the capital city now formed, your immediate goal should be to establish a military. Its job will be first to defend the city and then to explore. Note the Production window in the lower-right portion of the City screen seen in Figure 7.11. The default option in the Production window is for the city to allocate its resources toward building Militia units. Press Enter, and the

Figure 7.10: The city of Zimbabwe is founded as the Settlers move in

Main Game screen will reappear, allowing you to move the existing Cavalry unit (to explore) during the next group of turns, while Zimbabwe (your city) builds new Militia units.

Developing New Knowledge

In addition to building City Improvements, your civilization's Science Advisors will constantly work to develop new knowledge. The direction of that knowledge, however, is entirely your choice. From time to time, the Science Advisor will check in with you to report their progress.

When new knowledge is acquired, you must assign the scientists to a new task. (See Figure 7.12.) Each newly acquired knowledge leads to the ability to acquire even more new knowledge and to build more advanced City Improvements, additional Wonders of the World and better military units.

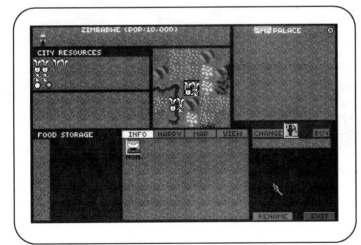

Figure 7.11: Zimbabwe's City screen shows that Militia units will be created

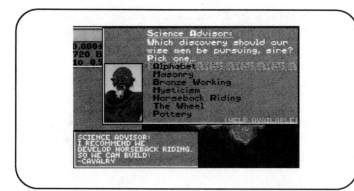

Figure 7.12: Select which new knowledge your Scientists should pursue

Because this is the first time the Science Advisor has appeared, you must decide now the path of knowledge you wish to pursue. Which great knowledge can be acquired later is determined by your initial choices. For example, to build additional Cavalry units (horseback military units, which are more powerful than Militia units), the Scientists must first acquire Horseback Riding. To build Chariots (also strong military units) knowledge of the Wheel must first be obtained.

For this tutorial, the scientists were assigned to obtain the knowledge of Pottery. It could take several turns after you assign the scientists the task of acquiring a new knowledge for the discovery to take place.

Continuing to Explore and to Build a Military

Meanwhile, the city (now represented by a square graphic icon containing a number) stands alone. A sole Cavalry unit provides your civilization's protection. Moving this Cavalry unit during each turn allows you to continue your exploration. Thus, two major things are now taking place in the Zulu empire: Zimbabwe is building up a military by creating Militia units, while the Cavalry

unit (acquired in the merger) is exploring new territory with each
passing turn. (Figure 7.13 illustrates these events taking place.)

By the year 3680 BC, you will notice that the Zulu tribe's treasury
has increased and that the Cavalry unit's exploration of the area has
turned up yet another small tribe (a random terrain square icon, as
shown in Figure 7.14).

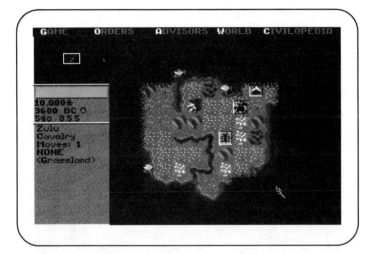

*Figure 7.13: The Calvary unit explores, while the city builds additional
military units*

Figure 7.14: The Calvary unit discovers another small tribe

Increasing the Treasury

Move the Cavalry unit onto the random icon's terrain square, and you will find that in this case, the Zulu tribe from Zimbabwe has discovered metal deposits, which will increase the tribe's treasury. The additional funds resulting from this discovery can be used by Zimbabwe to acquire an additional unit, or they can be saved in the treasury for future use, which is what we'll do in this case.

After another turn passes, the city of Zimbabwe has built its first Militia unit (Figure 7.15). Because metal deposits were discovered (and not spent), the treasury figure is now up to 105.

Protecting the City by Fortifying Military Units

To protect the city, you'll want to fortify the new Militia unit in a square next to the city.

Remember—fortifying a unit increases its defense strength by 50%.

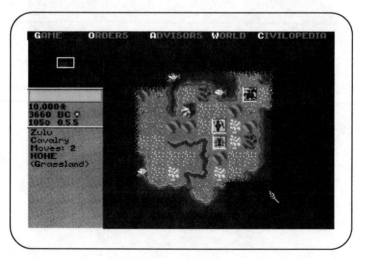

Figure 7.15: The city of Zimbabwe builds its first Militia unit

To fortify the Militia unit, select the Fortify option from the Orders pull-down menu. While a unit is being fortified, the letter "F" will appear within it until the fortification process is complete. In this case, when the new Militia unit became the active unit during the turn, it was moved one space outside of the city (as shown in Figure 7.16), and then it was fortified.

During this same turn, the Cavalry unit continued to explore.

While the Militia unit was being fortified, Zimbabwe continued to develop additional Militia units. (After the first Militia unit was created, no commands were given to change what the city should use its resources to build, so it built more Militia units.) Meanwhile, the Zulu scientists have announced that they have discovered the secret of Pottery.

Reallocating City Resources

If at this point you were to check the Change menu in the Production window (shown in Figure 7.17), you would see that you could now

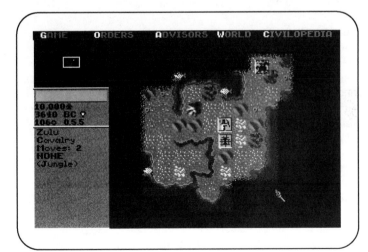

Figure 7.16: Zimbabwe's Militia unit is fortified to protect the city

Figure 7.17: Your scientists have discovered Pottery, so now a Granary can be built

decide to allocate the city's resources to building a Granary rather than Militia units.

Once again, the Science Advisor asks which knowledge the Zulu scientists should pursue. Because you are playing at the Chieftain level (where help is offered), in the lower-left corner of the Main Game screen the advisor recommends developing the Wheel so that Chariots can be built. In this simulation, however, we will order the scientists to pursue Horseback Riding first. This is done by high-lighting the scientific advancement, "Horseback Riding," on the menu shown in Figure 7.18.

As mentioned before, when you are playing at the Chieftain level, help is offered in the form of on-screen messages advising you to make a certain move or decision. However, you don't *have* to take the advice—you can instead choose to employ any strategy you like.

Choosing the knowledge you will assign your scientists to pursue is a vital aspect of your strategy. Thus, to quickly discover what each early discovery will eventually lead to, check out the Science

Figure 7.18: Scientists are ordered to pursue the knowledge of Horseback Riding

Discovery charts in Chapter 9 of this book.

Checking Your Maps and Screens

As turns take place, the Cavalry unit continues to explore. You can see quickly how much land has been explored by checking out the small map in the upper-left corner of the Main Game screen. (Figure 7.19 shows the Main Game screen at this point in the simulation.) Within the square on the small map is the active unit. The other small dot on the map represents the city of Zimbabwe.

From the information just below the small map, you can see that the year is 3360 BC, that the Zulu's treasury is at 130, that the active unit is the Cavalry unit, and that the active unit is currently on a Forest terrain square. During this turn, the active Cavalry unit can move two spaces in any direction.

You can use the active unit(s) you have allocated for exploration (in this case, the Cavalry unit), to travel along the perimeter (coastline) of the land mass you occupy. This way, you can determine the size of the land mass and whether your civilization was founded on an island or large continent. If you discover your civilization is on a *small* island, you'll want to assign your scientists to follow a path of

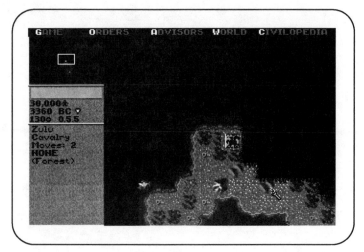

Figure 7.19: From the small map in the upper-left corner of the Main Game screen, you can see that as the Cavalary unit explores, more areas of the world are made visible

knowledge that will quickly lead to the ability to build different types of ships.

No matter what your ultimate goals in the game, you should make it a priority to discover Navigation (by obtaining the Alphabet and Map Making), so that you can explore the seas, establishing both trade routes and embassies.

Expansion of the Palace

Thus far in this simulation, the Zulu population has remained pleased with their leadership, so they've built an improvement to the Palace. When such an event takes place, you must decide which portion of the Palace you wish to expand. This choice is made from a separate game screen like the one in Figure 7.20.

To build onto the right side of the Palace or the left, select area 3 or 5. (In Figure 7.20, you will see that option 3 represents the left side of the

Figure 7.20: Decide which part of the Palace you want to improve

Palace.) To improve upon the Palace's entrance, choose area 4. To improve the grounds, select area A, B, and/or C.

To select which area of the Palace you wish to improve, simply press the appropriate number or letter on the keyboard.

After you choose the area of the palace you wish to improve upon, you must select the type of architecture to be used. You'll be given three choices, which are represented graphically. Once you've made your selection, the Palace addition will be built automatically (see Figure 7.21).

If you choose to improve the Palace grounds, the specific nature of the improvements (trees, fences, statues, etc.) will be determined by the computer.

Following your selections, a short animation sequence will show the improvement being made to the Palace (see Figure 7.22). After the animation sequence, game play will resume.

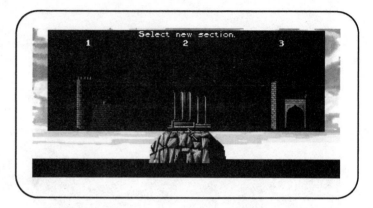

Figure 7.21: Select which type of architecture to use

Figure 7.22: The first Palace addition gets built

By now, many turns have taken place and the city of Zimbabwe has built several Militia units, a few of which are fortified and guard the city.

When a unit is fortified, it will be surrounded by a border, made up of a dashed line.

Expand and Develop
Your Civilization: 3200 BC

As time has passed (turns have taken place), Scientists have discovered the knowledge of Horseback Riding. The year is now 3200 BC, and the Zulu population is up to 60,000 citizens. As seen in Figure 7.23, five Militia units have been created; four of them have been fortified to protect the city of Zimbabwe.

Expanding Your Civilization

You must constantly expand your civilization by building new cities. To build additional cities, access the City screen for Zimbabwe and double-click on the Change button in the Production window. This will allow you to reallocate the city's resources and create an additional group of Settlers.

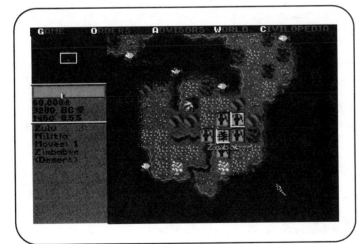

Figure 7.23: Four fortified Militia units now protect the city of Zimbabwe; an additional (inactive) Militia unit can explore

Figure 7.24: Double-click on the Change icon in the City screen to reallocate a city's resources toward building a different type of unit, a City Improvement, or a Wonder of the World

Notice that when the Change icon is activated, a menu asking "What shall we build in Zimbabwe?" appears. As your scientific knowledge improves and basic City Improvements are built, the list of possibilities increases. This menu (shown in Figure 7.24) lists those improvements your civilization has the knowledge to build, and offers information about the number of turns it will take to build each one.

Buying Improvements

To speed up the process, you can spend a portion of the treasury to *buy* an improvement. To do this, click on the Buy icon (near the Change icon) and the improvement's price will be displayed. If you choose to spend the funds, you will acquire the improvement during the next turn.

In this simulation, Zimbabwe was assigned to develop additional Settler units, to be used to establish new cities.

Navigating through the Copy-Protection Quiz

At this point, approximately fifty turns have taken place in the simulation, which means that the game's copy-protection scheme will become activated and a Civilization Copy-Protection Quiz (see Figure 7.25) will take place. The Copy-Protection Quiz helps MicroProse Software ensure that their software is not being *pirated* (illegally duplicated and distributed).

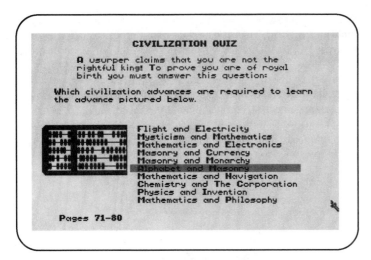

Figure 7.25: The Civilization Copy-Protection Quiz

To continue, you'll need the original Civilization manual, which was packaged with the game. The Quiz screen will pose a question, and refer to specific pages in the manual. Flip through the specified pages—in this case between pages 71 and 80—and look for the icon shown on screen—in this case, the abacus icon.

When you find the icon, you discover the answer to the Quiz question—in our example, that the Alphabet and Masonry advances are required to learn the Mathematics advance that was graphically depicted using the abacus icon as a clue.

If you answer the quiz question correctly (you have two chances), game play continues.

Saving the Game (and Continuing to Play)

Because the default Autosave option was selected (from the Game menu and then the Options pull-down menu), the computer will periodically save this simulation's game data. (See Figure 7.26.)

When the Autosave feature was activated, you were asked where (on which disk drive) you wanted the data stored. The default option was drive C: (the hard disk), which contains the MPS subdirectory.

To save the game data and continue now, press Enter. That way, if you make drastic mistakes in later turns, you can end the simulation, reload the current game data, and start again from this point in the game.

If you prefer to skip saving the game information and immediately return to game play, press Esc (the Escape key).

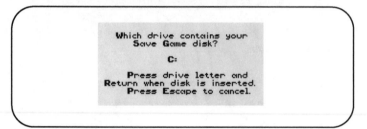

Figure 7.26: When the AutoSave option is activated, the game data is saved automatically to disk

Continuing to Develop: 2800 BC

The year is now 2800 BC and a second city, Ulundi, has been created by the group of Settlers formed by Zimbabwe. Units that were assigned to explore the land have discovered that the Zulu tribe is based on a rather small island. Meanwhile, the resources of Ulundi have been assigned to build Chariot units while the city of Zimbabwe continues to build new Settler units. Ulundi's City screen is shown in Figure 7.27.

The Tribe Pursues Many Tasks

The Zulu empire is doing several things at once, as each city's resources are allocated to accomplish separate tasks—which should ultimately help the empire as a whole achieve its goals.

The Zulu tribe now consists of two cities. To quickly assess progress, press Alt+A to access the Advisors menu (Figure 7.28).

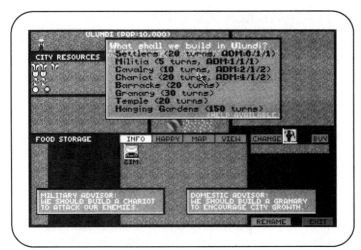

Figure 7.27: The city of Ulundi is formed and is assigned to build Chariot units

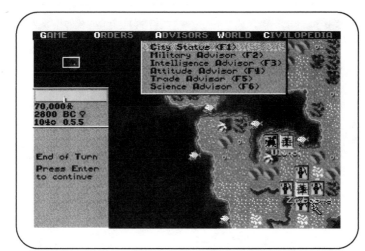

Figure 7.28: Check in with your Advisors through the Advisors pull-down menu

Getting Reports from Your Advisors

Pressing F6 allows you to request a report from the Science Advisor, who states that the scientists are researching the knowledge of Bronze Working, and that by the current year (2800 BC) the Zulu empire has already acquired the knowledge of Pottery, Horseback Riding, the Wheel, Ceremonial Burial, and Masonry.

Notice (in Figure 7.29) that some of the items in this list are highlighted in white. These are basic topics of knowledge—the key building blocks from which you can expand your civilization's knowledge.

By once again pressing ALT+A for the Advisors menu, but this time pressing F2, you can check in with the Military Advisor. In the Military Advisor's report (Figure 7.30) for this simulation, you will be informed that one group of settlers is being developed in Zimbabwe, and one Chariot unit is being built in Ulundi, while a total of

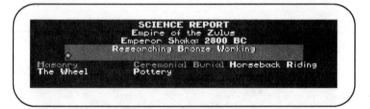

Figure 7.29: The Science Advisor's report

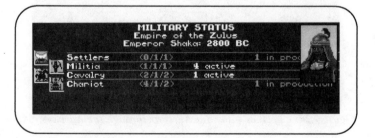

Figure 7.30: The Military Advisor's report

four active Militia units and one active Cavalry unit now make up the civilization's military.

The Civilization Expands Further

Multiple turns have taken place, and the simulation continues to progress. Zimbabwe has created another group of Settlers and they have formed a new city (the third in the Zulu empire), called Bapedi. Now that Bapedi has been founded, it is necessary to assign it with a building task (Figure 7.31).

Notice that the menu of available improvements has grown, because the Zulu empire has acquired additional knowledge.

From the Main Game screen shown in Figure 7.32, it's easy to see that the Zulu population has now grown to 100,000 people, and that Ulundi has built and fortified its first Chariot unit.

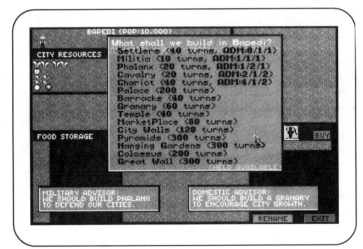

Figure 7.31: With the creation of a new city (Bapedi), you must determine what that new city should build

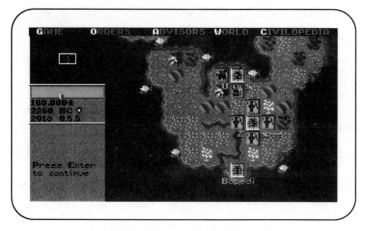

Figure 7.32: The Main Game screen allows you to see available units and where they are located

The Information Screen
Compares Your Civilization to Others

Civilization periodically provides an information screen, which appears automatically and offers you data comparing your civilization to others currently evolving on the planet. (These other civilizations are being controlled by the computer.) From this screen (shown in Figure 7.33), we now find out that in this simulation, the Zulu empire is the wealthiest on the planet.

An Expanding Civilization
Copes with Attack: 1180 BC

By the year 1180 BC, the Zulu population has reached 200,000 and a total of six cities have been built (see Figure 7.34), although only Zimbabwe and Ulundi are properly protected from surprise invasions.

Toynbee completes his epic history:
'The WEALTHIEST Civilizations in the World'

1. The Glorious Civilization of the Zulus.

2. The Great Civilization of the Russians.

3. The Fine Civilization of the Germans.

Figure 7.33: The wealthiest civilizations in the world

Further Expansion

Zimbabwe continues to build new groups of Settlers, while Ulundi continues to build Chariot units. Checking in with the Science Advisor reveals that it is possible to see how well the Zulu civilization is progressing (from a knowledge and technology standpoint).

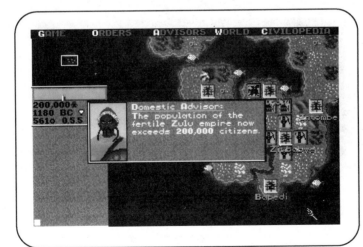

Figure 7.34: The Zulu tribe's population continues to expand

Coping with Barbarian Raids

Among the most frustrating obstacles you'll encounter during a simulation are barbarian raids. These random attacks just can't be prevented. At best, you can *anticipate* a raid by being prepared with a good defense.

In this simulation, two barbarian cavalry units and one barbarian leader now initiate an attack on the unprotected city of Intombe. (The barbarian icons are red when they appear on the Main Game screen, as shown in Figure 7.35.)

By the time a Chariot unit from Ulundi could be activated (from Fortified status) and moved toward Intombe, the city was invaded and captured by the barbarians. The result was the loss of that city as well and a decrease in the treasury.

Of course, this attack could have been avoided easily if the city of Intombe had been protected by at least two or three military units.

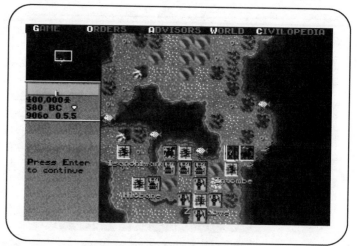

Figure 7.35: Barbarians raid the Zulu civilization

Despite the fact that the Zulu empire lost the city of Intombe to the barbarians, the Chariot unit from Ulundi managed to capture the barbarian leader and a handsome ransom is paid (Figure 7.36).

Whenever barbarians raid, they always have a leader. If you can capture the leader, your empire will receive a ransom fee. To receive the ransom, it is important that the barbarian leader be alone (not protected by another unit) when he is captured. It is also possible to defeat both the barbarians and their leader in one attack (if they are sharing a terrain square), but then both units will be destroyed and no ransom will be paid.

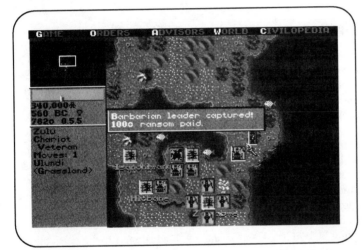

Figure 7.36: Ulundi's Chariot leader captures the barbarian leader and a ransom is paid

A Thriving Civilization: 140 BC

As the year 140 BC arrives, the Zulu empire is stable, although not growing quickly. A check with the Science Advisor (Figure 7.37) reveals twenty different knowledges that have been acquired (by the scientists, or through the discovery of secret scrolls, or through winning battles).

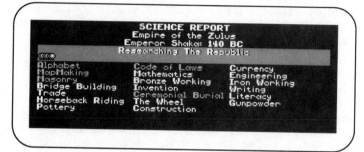

Figure 7.37: A quick check-in with the Science Advisor shows which knowledges your empire has acquired thus far

Tips for Continuing a Successful Simulation

By now, each of the existing cities within the Zulu civilization is developing some type of City Improvement or Wonder of the World—for example, one city continues to generate Settlers for continued expansion, while another city builds military units to protect the empire.

During your simulations, you'll want to assign tasks to each city that will help you in reaching the goal(s) you have set. Based on these goals, you must develop strategies, often taking into account several things at once. For example, one city could be dealing with a surprise attack by barbarians who have arrived by boat, another city could be building a Wonder of the World, and several more cities might be building Caravan units to lend support to the cities building wonders. Meanwhile, you may have a military unit, Caravan, and Diplomat exploring the seas via a Sailing Vessel, looking to set up trading routes and an embassy with a foreign empire.

During each turn, you must allocate the appropriate resources to each of these endeavors, while determining the immediately appropriate action(s) of each active unit.

When a city (such as Isandhlwana) is located near the water, it is difficult to protect it from barbarians or enemies that attack from the water. (Water-borne attacks such as the one shown in Figure 7.38 are common.) Building a City Wall around the city is your best defense; however, this takes resources and special knowledges.

Until your empire has established a navy (or at least built boats) you won't be able to get a good view of what lies in the water. If the waters near Isandhlwana had been explored by the Zulus, the barbarian attack would not have been a surprise—Zulu military units could have been waiting on land to defend the city.

Remember, early in this simulation, the city of Zimbabwe was commanded to stop generating Settlers and to build its first City Improvement. After several turns, a Granary was built and an animated graphic sequence (Figure 7.39) was shown on the screen.

In the middle or later portions of a simulation, a city could contain a dozen or more City Improvements and/or a few Wonders of the World. As a specific city grows, it is vital that you protect that city against disasters and sudden attacks. After all, you would not want a wonder to be lost or a trade route destroyed if a key city were suddenly raided.

To protect a key city, build a City Wall. Around the city, you should also fortify the most modern type of military unit(s) you have. A well-managed city with established trade routes and a handful of City Improvements will bring in extra income, which will allow you to achieve knowledge faster.

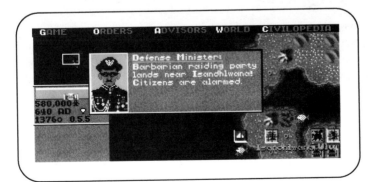

Figure 7.38: Barbarians launch a surprise attack from the sea

Figure 7.39: The city of Zimbabwe builds its first City Improvement—a Granary

The following two Civilization screens (Figures 7.40 and 7.41) represent a well-rounded and established city. This city was created during a different simulation from the one we have been pursuing in this chapter, but it shows what can be done in one city within a civilization that is made up of multiple cities and dozens of units.

Moving Along

By now you should have a basic understanding of how to establish a capital city and start an ongoing growth pattern. Completing a simulation takes hundreds of turns with perhaps thousands of individual decisions. No two simulations can be identical, so a step-by-step guide wouldn't help much here.

As your own simulation begins, keep in mind that everything works together or is somehow related. If you want to develop Flight (an early step toward space travel), some of the major knowledge

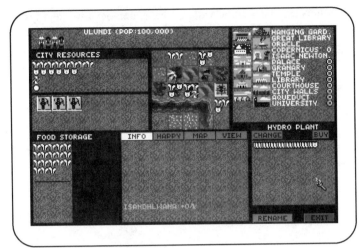

Figure 7.40: In a well-developed city, the City Improvements window in the upper-right corner of the screen is nearly full

Figure 7.41: This city, which has many City Improvements and several Wonders of the World, is also protected by City Walls

advancements that must be acquired are: Ceremonial Burial, Mysticism, Astronomy, Navigation, and Physics. Only after all of these major knowledge advancements have been acquired can scientists offer your civilization the knowledge of Flight.

This may sound complicated, but by referring to the charts in Chapter 9, you can outline the advances in knowledge that will help your civilization build the appropriate City Improvements.

Chapter 8 will introduce some general and specific strategies for winning Civilization.

Chapter 8

Civilization Strategies and Quick Tips

To finish a simulation successfully, you must achieve one of two
ultimate goals: conquer the world, or colonize Alpha Centauri (in
space). One of these goals must be chosen when you establish your
capital city. Then, to achieve your goal, you have to create a
workable plan, and make progress as the "years" (turns) go on. Your
decisions and actions during each turn will determine your empire's
destiny.

How You Can Benefit
from the Experience of Other Players

Unfortunately, there is no predetermined path to ensure your empire's
success, so the best way to judge the potential success of your
strategy is to examine what has worked (and what hasn't) during
other simulations.

As mentioned before, a simulation can take many hours—you can
use the game's Autosave option (or manual Save) to save the game
data periodically, then take excellent advantage of this feature by
restarting the simulation from the point at which it was last saved, if
that point was *before* an unexpected problem arose. (As an example,
if you were planning to launch a major invasion, you could save the
game data before the attack. Then, if your invasion didn't go as
planned, you could restart the simulation and try a different approach.)

Interact with Other Civilization Players

Various on-line services, including CompuServe, America OnLine,
Prodigy, and the MicroProse BBS (bulletin board system), offer
interactive computer game forums where players can share their
experiences and exchange information about their favorite games.
Civilization has a large following of game players dedicated to
discovering new ways to create and manage successful Civilization
empires. In this chapter, you'll find their detailed strategies and tips,

which have been culled from postings on the on-line Civilization forums.

Sample Strategies and Game Strategy Tips

This section outlines a few overall strategies and tips that other Civilization players have discovered and made available through on-line services. You can incorporate these strategies in your own simulations. These strategies and tips are not listed in any particular order; you can incorporate the information within them that pertains to your personal Civilization goals as you wish.

To access an on-line service, you'll need an optional modem and modem software, as well as an "account" for the on-line service.

Conquering the World:
A Step-by-Step Strategy

This strategy was developed for the Emperor level of a simulation and is intended to conquer the world.

By the year 1880 AD, the player who created this strategy had managed to conquer the world and receive a rating of 123%. (The percentage rating mentioned is one of the ways Civilization measures your success as a leader. See Chapter 12 for more details on scoring.) To achieve the goals mentioned, it was necessary to restore from a saved game on three occasions, after unexpected disasters or barbarian raids had taken place.

Implementing the Strategy

At the start of the simulation (after the pre-game choices were made), the Tax Rate was set to 100% Science. Two Militia units were created and then fortified to protect the capital city.

Once the simulation was underway and the first several turns had taken place, the Scientists were instructed to research the Wheel and then Pottery. All funds were invested in research until these two knowledge advances were discovered.

The preceding portion of the strategy took approximately 42 turns to achieve (and might have taken longer if other technologies were discovered through the finding of Ancient Scrolls or through military force).

Moving on in the simulation, a second Militia unit was created, and then a few turns passed before the discovery of Pottery and the knowledge of the Wheel allowed for the building of Chariots (which can be used for exploration). During that time, Barracks were built within the capital city to give the existing military units added strength.

You can always reallocate the city's resources from the City screen by using the Change option.

The first step in exploration was to locate the coastline and explore it. For now, the player left untouched random squares (hut icons) that were close to the capital city or any other city (exploring these random squares might have released barbarians).

Chariot units are also vital for protecting the city against attack and for defeating other empires. Using Chariot units to invade foreign cities early in the game offers a very high chance of success, because newly founded cities are usually guarded by only a few Militia units, which a Chariot can defeat easily.

Conquering Rival Cities

One key to the success of *this* strategy was to quickly conquer *all* rival cities located on the same continent as the player's capital city.

Taking the offense by using Chariot units and other military units to launch attacks (as opposed to signing peace treaties or otherwise coexisting with other civilizations) is an excellent way to acquire world dominance. When following this strategy, you should explore only those random squares near foreign cities, because if you unleash barbarians, they may actually help you by destroying the foreign cities.

After one or two Chariot units were built for exploration and invading foreign cities on the same continent, the resources of the capital city were allocated to building additional groups of Settlers, which led to the formation of additional cities within the player's empire.

After enough time passed for the scientists to research and discover Pottery, the Tax Rate was adjusted to 50/50 between tax and science, and the knowledge of Bronze Working was sought. Granaries (allowed by the knowledge of Pottery) were built in each city for food storage.

Meanwhile, the Scientists were hard at work seeking technological advances, and the Chariot units were exploring and attacking any rival cities they encountered.

This is just one example of how a player must oversee several tasks at once during a simulation.

Once Barracks were built in one city, they were used to create Phalanx units. Each city was then fortified with at least one Phalanx unit.

Uncovering Random Squares

Remember those random squares that were temporarily left untouched? Now, with Phalanx units protecting the cities and Chariot units in the field, Militia units were sent to explore the random squares that were previously passed by.

Should you unleash barbarians, it is no great loss if your Militia units are conquered, because Militia units are cheap to create and will represent no great loss to the empire. Other military units, if lost, would take time and resources to rebuild.

If a random square is more then ten squares away from one of your Civilization's cities, there is little danger if barbarians are unleashed, because they don't seem to travel far.

In this strategy, Chariot units were the military force behind conquering the continent. Once the continent was under the player's empire's total control, all of the empire's resources were allocated to expansion, through the building of Settlers and Phalanx units.

Catapult units are also excellent for defense. They can successfully weather attacks by many other military units. Also if you launch a Catapult unit attack, it has a high chance of success.

Continuing in the strategy, as expansion took place, the scientists were assigned to pursue Pyramids. Had another civilization discovered Pyramids first, the Observatory would have been a good second choice. All of the other ancient Wonders of the World were ignored.

See Chapter 6 for an explanation of the advantages of these specific choices.

After the Pyramids (or Observatory) were acquired, Religion was acquired, and Michelangelo's Chapel was pursued.

When selecting Wonders of the World to build, two options are to develop the Colossus wonder early on and to build Courthouses. Then, when you later change the form of government to the Republic, your empire will acquire Lightbulb icons (scientific development power) much faster, and future advancements in knowledge will happen more quickly.

Once you have established Trade, it is useful for cities to build Caravans and to have the Caravan units travel to those cities that are building wonders in order to lend support. This can greatly speed up the process for building Wonders of the World, and is the only method by which one city can assist another in development.

As the middle portion of the sample strategy was reached, the scientists continued to pursue the more modern Wonders of the World, including Newton's College, Bach's Cathedral and Magellan's Expedition. As soon as the empire had the ability to pursue the most modern wonders (such as the Apollo Program), resources were dedicated toward those goals instead of the soon-to-be-outmoded wonders.

In the sample strategy, Women's Suffrage was the most important wonder in the later stages of the game—this Wonder of the World made it possible to mobilize a modern offensive while still maintaining a Republic.

Options for Continuing

The SETI Program and Hoover Dam might also be important wonders, especially if the civilization were on a large continent. After obtaining these wonders, the Cure for Cancer should be sought after. Then, the player could go back and obtain whatever other Wonders of the World remain from the Middle Ages.

Once you're in the modern era, you can always go back and develop less advanced wonders, since you already have obtained the knowledges required to build them.

From a technological standpoint, your civilization should pursue the Railroad and Conscription early on.

Masonry, Construction and Bridge Building are the major knowledge advancements required to build Railroads. See the charts in Chapter 9 for further details.

After the Railroad is obtained, each city on the home continent should be connected via Railroad before any units attempt to explore or attack beyond the home continent.

Riflemen and Ironclad units are important defenses as the simulation progresses.

After the home continent is conquered, and when the time comes to expand further, the player can build Temples and Cathedrals and will want to change the form of leadership (which will still have been set to the default option of despotism unless it was changed by the player).

Before the player can enter a Democracy, but after the Pyramids have been obtained, the government can be changed to a Republic or Monarchy as needed, without having to enter a state of Anarchy.

The player's goal will be to change to a Democracy as soon as possible.

Moving Along in the Sample Simulation

At this point (very close to the modern era), the Scientists were allocated to work toward obtaining Robotics and then building Manufacturing Plants in all of the major cities. Now—because the player continued to gain knowledge and build City Improvements and Wonders of the World—the empire has grown strong and large enough to spread outward to other continents.

The player built as many Bombers as possible and switched to a Republic when the population started to become unhappy. At this point, Women's Suffrage was an absolute must!

As an empire grows, it becomes more difficult to keep the population happy, although the player might not be doing anything wrong in particular.

The player also built Carriers, Transports, and Battleship units to begin a conquest of foreign continents. First, a Diplomat was sent to determine the strength of the enemy, then Battleships were sent to destroy any foreign coastal cities that did not have City Walls. Once the coastal cities were beaten, the army (made up of Riflemen and other military units) was loaded into Carriers and Transports, and sent across seas to invade foreign continents.

As Riflemen invaded the foreign beaches, and reached enemy cities, they were temporarily fortified. The player started the attack by blasting each rival city with Bombers until its defenses were worn down, then sent in ground-based Riflemen troops.

You may also want to develop and send along Artillery to assist in a ground-based assault.

The player repeated this procedure on foreign continents, conquering them one at a time, until worldwide domination was achieved.

Overall, about 80% of your resources should be allocated throughout the game toward the development of technology, which has bearing on military strength. Using the military you develop in this way will be a key toward obtaining world domination (and winning the game).

While the sample strategy presented here for conquering the world is sound, your personal decisions combined with random events during each turn may result in varying results. With practice, using this overall strategy combined with the tips and strategies that follow will ultimately lead to your success.

Keeping Your Population Happy

Especially when you are playing at the Emperor level, one of the most difficult tasks you face is maintaining the happiness of the population. Developing Religion—and later the Bach's Cathedral and Michelangelo's Chapel Wonders of the World—will help you maintain happiness.

One of the major differences between the various skill levels in Civilization is how easily the population can be kept happy rather than content or unhappy.

Another Conquer-the-World Strategy

When playing at the Chieftain level with seven civilizations on the planet, one overall strategy is to build the Colossus as early in the game as possible after the capital city is founded and protected.

Next, increase trade for that city so that the city's wealth and its scientific efforts will increase. Keep building up the capital city until the number in the center of the capital city box (on the main game screen) reaches four.

Then, create Settlers and have them build additional cities and roads between the cities.

From a military standpoint, you'll want to build as many Chariot units as possible and use them to conquer your continent. This can be done now by establishing additional cities and allocating their resources toward building Chariots.

While this is taking place, have your scientists pursue the following advances (in this order):

1. Pottery (for building Granaries)
2. The Wheel (for Chariots and the construction of Aqueducts)
3. Bronze Working (for Phalanx defense units, Currency, and the Colossus wonder)
4. Sail (to be able to travel across the oceans and to obtain Magellan's Expedition wonder)
5. Invention (which leads to the Steam Engine and the ability to build Ironclads, Railroads, and Gunpowder)
6. Railroad (to increase food and resources for cities connected with a rail system, and to obtain Darwin's Voyage)
7. Gunpowder (for Musketeers)
8. Electronics (which leads to the Hoover Dam wonder and the Hydro Plant improvement)
9. Banking
10. Automobile
11. Mass Production
12. Communism and Labor Unions (which allow for Mechanized Infantry)

With the Mechanized Infantry units you will develop, your civilization will have an excellent defense rating (6), a strong offense rating (6), and a rating that indicates the ability to travel quickly during turns (3) when launching attacks.

Expanding without Using Military Force

Diplomats are an inexpensive way to steal technology and knowledge from rival cities and overthrow the rival cities without launching a military attack.

If you can conquer rivals without violence, you can allocate your empire's resources to other tasks than building a strong military. In the scheme of the next conquer-the-world strategy presented, this strategy (using both peaceful methods and warring techniques) leads to success.

Conquer the World: Take Three

After selecting a tribe (in this example, the Aztecs were chosen) and establishing the capital city, immediately build a second city. Then have scientists develop the Wheel.

Now, allocate the second city's resources to the nonstop building of Chariot units. Meanwhile, the capital city should build Settlers, so that new cities can be established and more Chariot units can be built.

Set the tax rate to 100% science, and keep developing Chariot units. Begin to explore your continent and take over any rival cities on the continent. Once you have totally established your domination on your continent, build additional cities and have the Scientists start pursuing Sail and Trade. (Build a few Trireme units and then Sail ships, when possible.)

You'll also want to build additional cities, which you can dedicate to developing Wonders of the World. As you develop the ability to travel the seas, start building Diplomats.

Now, load the boats with military units and a Diplomat, and start to explore the world, one continent at a time. When you encounter a rival city, launch an attack with Chariot units. You can use Diplomats to steal technology and weaken a rival city's defenses. As you take over foreign cities, have them develop additional Chariots. Use Sail and other sea vessels to explore the water and constantly transport military units and Diplomats to new areas. (You'll want to explore the entire world.)

As long as you dedicate at least 75% of your total resources to building up a military (made up of Chariots) and start launching attacks early in the game, you will find that expanding your civilization will be easy.

The more rival civilizations you conquer early in the game, the easier it will be to take over the entire world. Once you become the world leader, your accomplishment will make headlines (as shown in Figure 8.1), and foreign leaders will acknowledge your power (Figure 8.2).

Your simulation will end, and you'll be graded on your leadership abilities (Figure 8.3).

As you build up your military, it is important to establish some cities that will be dedicated to building Wonders of the World.

Figure 8.1: When you conquer all rival civilizations, your accomplishments will make newspaper headlines

Figure 8.2: When you become the world leader, each of the rival civilization's leaders will acknowledge defeat

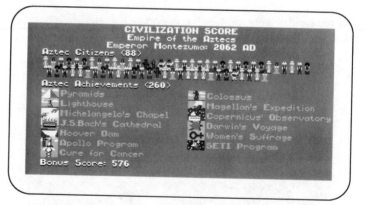

Figure 8.3: At the conclusion of a simulation, your score will be displayed, along with information about which Wonders of the World you have acquired

You can achieve the two ultimate goals of the game in one simulation. When you have conquered all but one civilization, allow that final rival to maintain one city (so the game won't end), but surround that city with your fortified military units, and don't allow it to expand. Then, reallocate your cities toward pursuing space travel. Other than occasional barbarian attacks, you won't have to worry about maintaining a strong defense, because you have captured just about the entire world. Your quest for space should now be easy.

Civilization Strategy Tidbits

The following strategy tidbits can be incorporated into your own strategies as needed.

Use Diplomats to Steal Technology and Wonders

If, in the Medieval Age, your army is made up primarily of Knights and Cannons, it is difficult to successfully attack more advanced cities that are defended by armored infantry. To overcome this disadvantage, create Diplomats and have them steal every technological advance they can from rival empires.

You can even steal Wonders of the World and should concentrate on obtaining J.S. Bach's Cathedral, Women's Suffrage and the Hoover Dam. In short, if you don't have the time or resources to build wonders, steal them!

A Low-Expansion, High-Exploration Strategy

One player started the game as a Warlord and did nothing but create armies and expand, with 0% tax and 100% science. No additional roads or Settler units were created (thus no additional cities, other than the capital city) were built. By the year 2100, this strategy allowed for 40,000 Settlers to travel into space.

Cheating in Civilization

At the start of a simulation, most of the territory around your capital city is unexplored (it appears to be black). If you are using version 1 or 2 of Civilization, you can get an overview of the entire planet and see inside enemy cities. When you're at the main game screen, hold down the left Shift key and press: **1 2 3 4 5 6 7 8 9 0 t**. Then double-click on the small entire world map in the upper-left portion of the screen.

This will put you into the game's "cheat mode" (which is only available in versions 1 and 2 of Civilization). To exit this mode, repeat the same procedure.

You can also randomize the leaders of the other civilizations—while in "cheat mode," press ALT+R.

For other methods of "cheating" in Civilization, check out Chapter 9.

Accepting Peace Treaties Lets You Grow Internally

Early in the simulation—as you are building up your empire's military and resources—accept all treaty and peace offers from rival civilizations. Treaties can always be broken later, when you're ready to launch an attack. In the meantime, having treaties will help to maintain peace, so you can concentrate on building up your civilization.

Your rivals can also break treaties and launch attacks. This doesn't happen often, but when it does, you can usually see the attacks coming.

Build a Navy to Guard Your Coastline

Once you can build boats and other vessels, use them to guard your coastline cities from enemy attacks originating from the sea. City Walls will also help protect cities near the water, but will not stop surprise attacks from rival civilizations or barbarians.

More on Keeping Your Population Happy

If you're having trouble maintaining happy citizens, build plenty of luxuries and allocate members of the population to be Entertainers. Certain City Improvements and Wonders of the World (especially those having to do with advanced knowledge such as Universities and Libraries, or Religion) will go a long way toward keeping your people happy. You can also lower the Tax Rate and raise the Luxury Rate. If you offer your citizens an abundance of luxuries, you can expect a "We Love the King" day to be declared in each city containing a happy population.

Building Irrigation on Terrain Squares

When it comes to founding new cities, keep in mind that you can only irrigate terrain squares that are near sources of water (oceans, lakes, or rivers) or that are connected to cities that already have irrigation.

As a city expands internally, irrigation helps the citizens produce food of higher quality. When you establish a city on a Plains terrain square, be sure to irrigate that square first. This will enhance the square's ability to generate food, which can maintain a growing population.

Building Railroads

Building Railroads is an excellent improvement to any civilization. Railroads allow military units to be transported easily. A 50% bonus (in the form of Trade, resource, and food production) is given to cities connected via a rail system.

When to Speak with Foreign Diplomats

You should always take the time to speak with foreign diplomats, unless your civilization is governed as a Republic or Democracy. Under those governments, your senate will automatically accept any treaties, and you may not be able to break them later without a vote.

Reach for the Stars (and Colonize Them)

If your goal in a simulation is to explore and colonize space, you *must* plan to obtain the Apollo Program Wonder of the World as early as possible, because building and successfully launching a spaceship can take several decades.

Space Travel and Colonization

After obtaining the Apollo Program wonder, enter the City screen for any of your cities and double-click on the Change button. Notice that there are three additional menu options, which represent three types of *pieces* from which spaceships can be built. The three menu options are:

- SS (Space Ship) Structural
- SS Component
- SS Module

Each of these three pieces will be described in detail later in this section.

The Apollo Program gave your civilization the *knowledge* to build
· spaceships. Now, dedicate as many cities in your Civilization as possible to building these three pieces, so that a complete spaceship can eventually be built and launched.

Each civilization can only build, launch, and maintain one spaceship at a time. (After the spaceship lands or is destroyed another ship can be built.) Thus, all cities that are not performing vital tasks should be assigned to building *pieces* of a spaceship. Once the ship has been launched, cities can be reassigned so that their resources are directed toward internal improvements or to the development of other, yet undiscovered wonders.

You'll also notice that the Apollo Program knowledge (which presumably includes *satellites*) enables you to see the location of every rival city in the world, even if you haven't yet discovered the rival cities (see Figure 8.4).

Figure 8.4: The Apollo Program Wonder of the World is your gateway to space travel

Building a Spaceship

You must build a spaceship that will carry as many colonists as possible. This is done from a special game screen, as shown in Figure 8.5. Of course, a ship that carries more colonists needs more fuel and resources in order to complete the stellar journey safely.

For the journey, the spaceship must carry food, energy, propulsion, and fuel. Once again, all of these elements are related and together they will determine the speed and success rate of the voyage.

Each time one of the cities in your empire builds an SS Structural, SS Component, or SS Module unit, the Spaceship Game screen will appear and offer information about your pending space voyage.

An *SS* (spaceship) unit works very much like a City Improvement, but is applied to the spaceship that is being built.

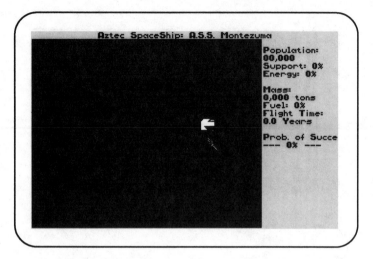

Figure 8.5: The Spaceship screen offers information vital to your interstellar voyage

On the right side of the Spaceship screen (in dialog boxes), the population allocated to the spaceship is displayed (in increments of 10,000 people). Without adequate Life Support and enough of an Energy Level to support the Life Support systems, the space travelers will not survive their journey. In the Spaceship screen dialog box, *Support* displays the spaceship's Life Support system in the form of a percentage, and *Energy Level* describes the amount of energy obtained, also in the form of a percentage.

Based on the ship's mass (size and weight), you will have to allocate enough Fuel and Propulsion to ensure that the ship will have power to reach its destination. Based on the Fuel and Propulsion allocated, the Flight Time of the ship will be displayed.

Each time an SS unit is added to the spaceship, the Life Support, Energy Level, and other related figures will change, which will affect the Probability of Success.

Prepare to Launch Your Spaceship

Because space travel is available to you only toward the end of the game, you'll want to make sure that Flight Time is as short as possible. (As you build your spaceship, make a mental note of the number of years remaining in the simulation.)

Before launching the spaceship (by double-clicking on the Launch icon at the bottom of the Spaceship screen), check that the Probability of Success is high and that the Flight Time is relatively low (under thirty years). If the Probability of Success is low, your space travelers might not survive the journey. Likewise, if the Flight Time is too long, the simulation could end before the spaceship reaches its destination (see Figure 8.6).

Remember—depending on the skill level you are using, your simulation will end in one of the following years:

| Chieftain: | 2100 AD |
| Warlord: | 2080 AD |

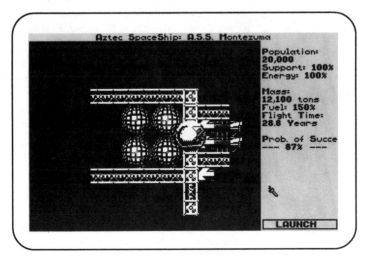

Figure 8.6: Before launching your spaceship, be sure that the Probability of Success is high and that the projected Flight Time is relatively short

Prince:	2060 AD
King:	2040 AD
Emperor:	2020 AD

In later "years" of the simulation, time passes in smaller increments—often one year at a time—so the seventy-year difference between the Chieftain and Emperor levels can make a huge difference.

Tips for Building a Better Spaceship

When building a spaceship, you must take into account each of the following additional considerations (which can be addressed by creating extra SS units):

Population	The number of people your spaceship is designed to carry.
Support	The percentage of the Population that can be supported on the journey through space, based on the available Life Support systems. (For example, if the ship's population is 20,000 but support is 50%, the ship's Life Support system can only sustain 10,000 people.)
Energy	The amount of energy required to maintain Life Support systems and other systems needed to maintain the spaceship's population.
Mass	Mass (the spaceship's size and weight) determines how much power, fuel and propulsion will be required for the ship to travel.
Fuel	The Fuel figure represents the amount of fuel already aboard the spaceship. Thus, if the Fuel indicator reads 60%, you will have to add 40% more fuel to fill the tanks.

Flight Time   Based on the spaceship's configuration, the computer will determine the number of years the space trek will take. (This figure will change as the ship's mass or engine power increase or decrease.)

Probability of Success   This figure tells you (based upon the food, life support, and resources available) the percentage of the ship's population that will live through the interstellar journey to colonize space.

SS Structural Units   Each time an SS Structural unit is added to the spaceship, the overall size of the ship increases. SS Structural units represent the basic shell of the ship, to which other components and modules can be attached. Without a sufficient number of SS Structural units, your spaceship can't hold other vital modules and components.

SS Component Units   Before attempting to build SS Component units, your civilization must have acquired the knowledge of Plastics. There are two basic types of Components: Propulsion and Fuel. Propulsion units represent the ship's engines and Fuel units then make the engines go. To make the ship travel faster, build extra Propulsion units. (Additional Fuel will be required to fuel the additional engine.)

SS Module Units   Now that the structure (shell) of the spaceship and its engines have been built, the ship requires Habitation modules, Life Support systems and Solar Panel modules to sustain its population on the long journey. Each time an SS Module is created by a city, you can select either a Habitation, Life Support, or Solar Panel module to be added to the ship.

(Building SS Modules requires the knowledge of Robotics.)

Each Habitation module or Life Support module will support 10,000 colonists, so plan and build your ship accordingly. Each Solar Panel can supply power to two other modules. So—if you have two Habitation modules and two Life Support Modules (for a total of four modules)—you'll also need to build two Solar Panel modules.

The Launch Countdown

When your ship is built and you're ready to launch it, double-click on the Launch button in the lower-right portion of the Spaceship screen. (Again, see Figure 8.6.)

Now the spaceship will travel toward its destination. In this case the journey will take approximately 28.8 years, during which time each city in the Aztec empire can build additional City Improvements, military units or Wonders of the World on the home planet to continue the empire's expansion and internal growth.

After the spaceship lands (or is destroyed) an additional spaceship can be built from scratch, which means the cities will have to build additional SS modules.

A spaceship will be destroyed if it runs out of fuel or if its energy is depleted before the spaceship reaches its destination. (See Figure 8.7.)

To make your spaceship travel at faster speeds, build at least two Propulsion units for each 10,000 colonists. Also, build your spaceship quickly—you want to be the first Civilization to reach Alpha Centauri. To raise additional funds to build SS units, you might consider selling some City Improvements. Once the spaceship is launched, you can always rebuild the City Improvements that were sold.

When you begin space exploration, have your planet-base scientists discover Future Technology Advances. These are worth five (5) points each, which will be added to your total game score.

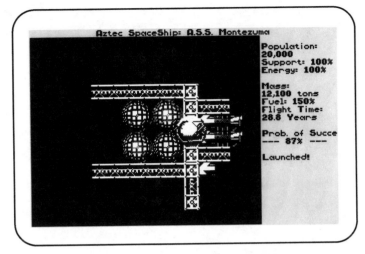

Figure 8.7: Provide your spaceship with everything it needs for a fast and safe journey

Your Space Travel Goal

Now that you've reached space, your goal is to reach Alpha Centauri and begin to establish colonies. Good luck, Godspeed, and

...may the force be with you

...and live long and prosper.

Chapter 9

Reference Charts

The charts in this chapter are meant to help you to create a strong military and build those Wonders of the World that will be most useful. You'll probably want to refer to these charts often during a simulation.

Wonders of the World: How to Obtain Them

There are two primary ways to obtain the twenty-one Wonders of the World, which (as you know by now) are important elements of this game. The first method is to *earn* each wonder by having your scientists develop the necessary knowledges and advances. The second method is for your civilization to *steal* them from other civilizations, by successfully invading and conquering any rival city that has obtained a wonder.

When Wonders Can Be Obtained

Wonders of the World are divided into three categories, based upon when—the *age*, or point in the game—they can be obtained. Within each age, seven wonders are available to be obtained or stolen.

Ancient Era

- Colossus
- Great Library
- Great Wall
- Hanging Gardens
- Lighthouse
- Oracle
- Pyramids

Medieval Age

- Copernicus's Observatory
- Darwin's Voyage
- Isaac Newton's College
- J.S. Bach's Cathedral
- Magellan's Expedition
- Michelangelo's Chapel
- Shakespeare's Theatre

Modern Times

- Apollo Program
- Cure for Cancer
- Hoover Dam
- Manhattan Project
- SETI Program
- Women's Suffrage
- United Nations

Advancement Charts for Wonders of the World

The following charts outline the necessary advances required to obtain each of the wonders available in the earlier times—the Ancient Era, and the Medieval Age.

In the early stages of the game, the seven wonders are relatively easy to obtain. Building them encourages you to assign your civilization's scientists to develop core knowledge that you will need later to create more advanced wonders. As you will see by examining these charts, many of the core knowledges—such as Alphabet, Ceremonial Burial, Bronze Working, the Wheel, Map Making, and Masonry—are prerequisites for many of the later wonders. Once your civilization has acquired a knowledge (like the Alphabet), you have it—you need not obtain that knowledge again.

These charts outline the key knowledges required to obtain each wonder, but *the order in which you achieve each of these knowledges may be slightly different.* The important thing is that your empire obtain each knowledge listed so that the civilization can acquire the wonder that follows.

As you acquire each of the knowledges required to build the Wonders of the World, you can also use the same knowledges to build various City Improvements. City Improvements help an individual city grow internally. Wonders of the World are built in individual cities, but they benefit the entire empire.

Wonders of the World: The Ancient Era

To obtain these early wonders, you must first assign your Scientists to obtain the following core knowledges: Pottery, Bronze Working, Alphabet, Code of Laws, Literacy, Masonry, Map Making, Ceremonial Burial, and Mysticism.

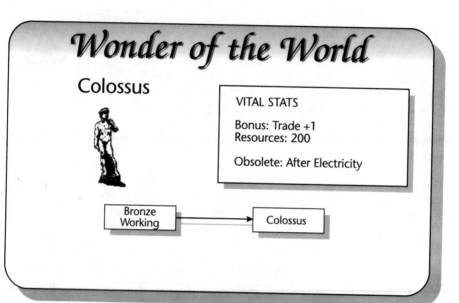

Wonder of the World

Colossus

VITAL STATS

Bonus: Trade +1
Resources: 200

Obsolete: After Electricity

Bronze Working → Colossus

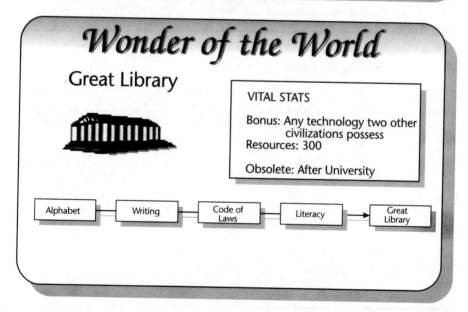

Wonder of the World

Great Library

VITAL STATS

Bonus: Any technology two other
civilizations possess
Resources: 300

Obsolete: After University

Alphabet → Writing → Code of Laws → Literacy → Great Library

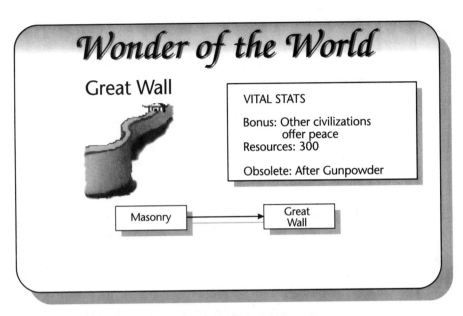

Wonder of the World

Great Wall

VITAL STATS

Bonus: Other civilizations offer peace

Resources: 300

Obsolete: After Gunpowder

Masonry → Great Wall

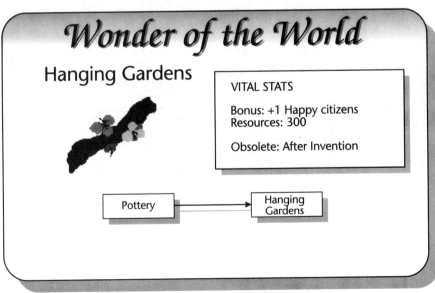

Wonder of the World

Hanging Gardens

VITAL STATS

Bonus: +1 Happy citizens
Resources: 300

Obsolete: After Invention

Pottery → Hanging Gardens

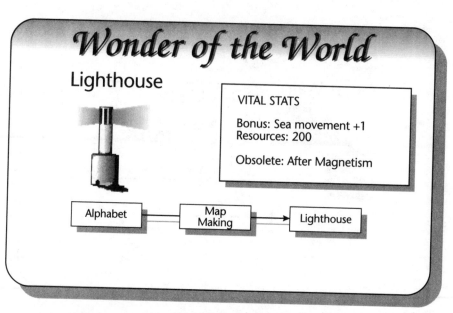

Wonder of the World
Lighthouse

VITAL STATS

Bonus: Sea movement +1
Resources: 200

Obsolete: After Magnetism

Alphabet → Map Making → Lighthouse

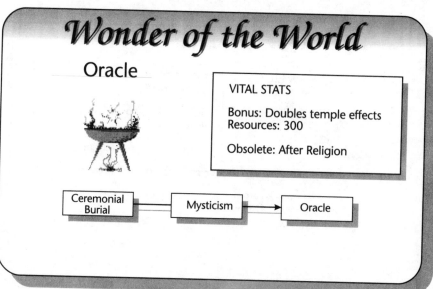

Wonder of the World
Oracle

VITAL STATS

Bonus: Doubles temple effects
Resources: 300

Obsolete: After Religion

Ceremonial Burial → Mysticism → Oracle

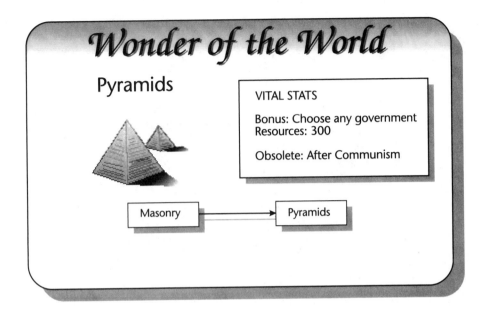

Wonder of the World

Pyramids

VITAL STATS

Bonus: Choose any government
Resources: 300

Obsolete: After Communism

Masonry → Pyramids

Wonders of the World: The Medieval Age

Those Wonders of the World that can be built in the Medieval Age are slightly more difficult to obtain—they require more advanced knowledge and take more turns and resources to build—for example, Darwin's Voyage requires your empire's Scientists to discover the Alphabet, Railroads, and Bridge Building.

As you reach the middle of the Medieval Age you should ensure that your civilization has acquired those basic knowledges that will be needed later to obtain quickly the more advanced wonders that become available when your civilization reaches Modern Times.

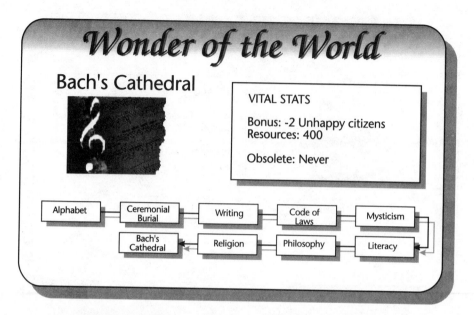

Wonder of the World

Bach's Cathedral

VITAL STATS

Bonus: -2 Unhappy citizens
Resources: 400

Obsolete: Never

```
Alphabet — Ceremonial — Writing — Code of — Mysticism
             Burial                  Laws
           Bach's   ← Religion ← Philosophy ← Literacy
           Cathedral
```

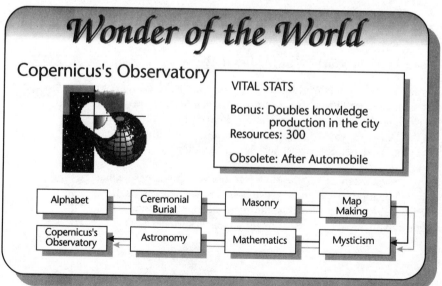

Wonder of the World

Copernicus's Observatory

VITAL STATS

Bonus: Doubles knowledge
         production in the city
Resources: 300

Obsolete: After Automobile

```
Alphabet — Ceremonial — Masonry — Map
             Burial                 Making
Copernicus's ← Astronomy ← Mathematics ← Mysticism
Observatory
```

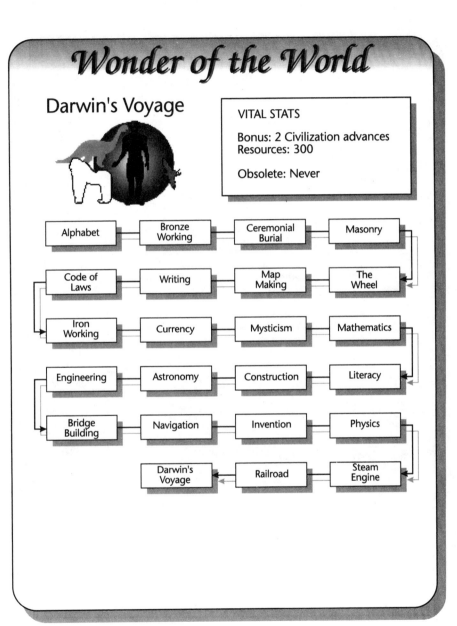

Wonder of the World

Darwin's Voyage

VITAL STATS

Bonus: 2 Civilization advances
Resources: 300

Obsolete: Never

Alphabet	Bronze Working	Ceremonial Burial	Masonry
Code of Laws	Writing	Map Making	The Wheel
Iron Working	Currency	Mysticism	Mathematics
Engineering	Astronomy	Construction	Literacy
Bridge Building	Navigation	Invention	Physics
Darwin's Voyage	Railroad		Steam Engine

Wonder of the World

Isaac Newton's College

VITAL STATS

Bonus: Increases production from Libraries and Universities
Resources: 400

Obsolete: After Nuclear Fission

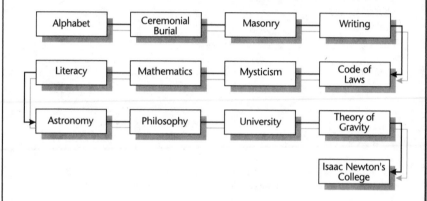

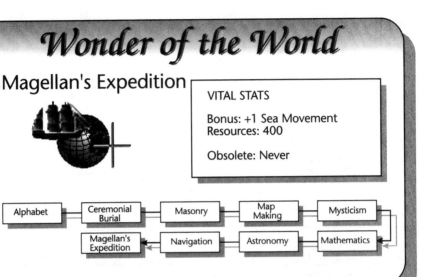

Wonder of the World

Magellan's Expedition

VITAL STATS

Bonus: +1 Sea Movement
Resources: 400

Obsolete: Never

| Alphabet | Ceremonial Burial | Masonry | Map Making | Mysticism |

| Magellan's Expedition | Navigation | Astronomy | Mathematics |

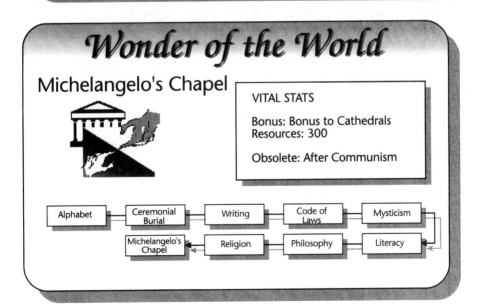

Wonder of the World

Michelangelo's Chapel

VITAL STATS

Bonus: Bonus to Cathedrals
Resources: 300

Obsolete: After Communism

| Alphabet | Ceremonial Burial | Writing | Code of Laws | Mysticism |

| Michelangelo's Chapel | Religion | Philosophy | Literacy |

Wonder of the World

Shakespeare's Theatre

VITAL STATS

Bonus: All unhappy citizens in the city are content
Resources: 400

Obsolete: After Electronics

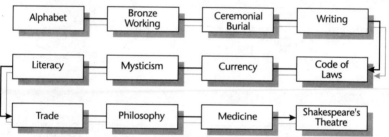

Alphabet	Bronze Working	Ceremonial Burial	Writing

Literacy	Mysticism	Currency	Code of Laws

Trade	Philosophy	Medicine	Shakespeare's Theatre

Wonders of the World: Modern Times

Acquiring the most advanced Wonders of the World, especially the Apollo Program and Women's Suffrage, will be key to winning the game.

In addition to the Modern Times Wonders of the World, there are also important City Improvements (called Future Technologies) that you will want to obtain. Future Technologies are worth an extra 5 points each toward your final game score. They are available only in later stages of a simulation, and represent technologies and improvements that have not yet been created in the real world.

Figure 9.1 Refer to the charts in this chapter for full details on the various Wonders of the World

Wonder of the World

Apollo Program

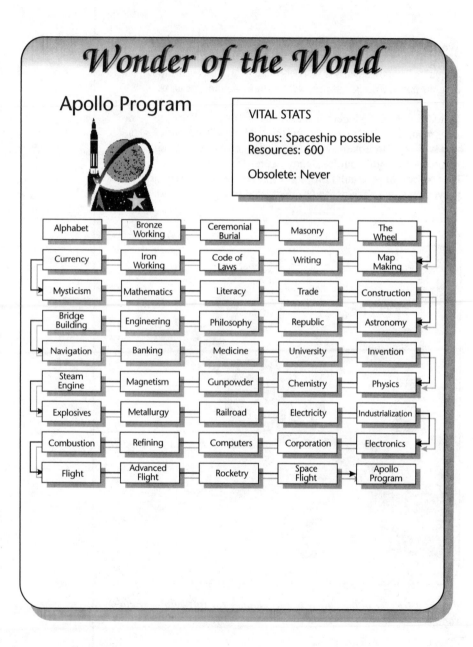

VITAL STATS

Bonus: Spaceship possible
Resources: 600

Obsolete: Never

Alphabet	Bronze Working	Ceremonial Burial	Masonry	The Wheel
Currency	Iron Working	Code of Laws	Writing	Map Making
Mysticism	Mathematics	Literacy	Trade	Construction
Bridge Building	Engineering	Philosophy	Republic	Astronomy
Navigation	Banking	Medicine	University	Invention
Steam Engine	Magnetism	Gunpowder	Chemistry	Physics
Explosives	Metallurgy	Railroad	Electricity	Industrialization
Combustion	Refining	Computers	Corporation	Electronics
Flight	Advanced Flight	Rocketry	Space Flight	Apollo Program

Cure for Cancer

VITAL STATS

Bonus: +1 Happy
Resources: 600

Obsolete: Never

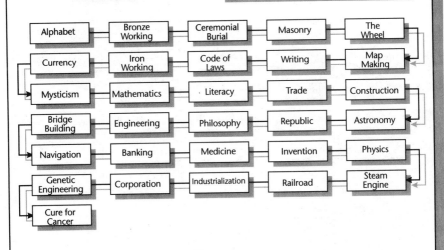

Alphabet	Bronze Working	Ceremonial Burial	Masonry	The Wheel
Currency	Iron Working	Code of Laws	Writing	Map Making
Mysticism	Mathematics	Literacy	Trade	Construction
Bridge Building	Engineering	Philosophy	Republic	Astronomy
Navigation	Banking	Medicine	Invention	Physics
Genetic Engineering	Corporation	Industrialization	Railroad	Steam Engine
Cure for Cancer				

Wonder of the World

Hoover Dam

VITAL STATS

Bonus: +50% Resources to each
       city on the continent
Resources: 600

Obsolete: Never

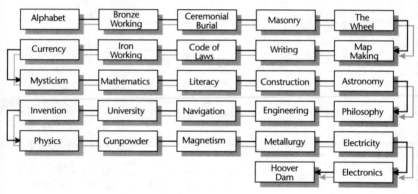

Alphabet	Bronze Working	Ceremonial Burial	Masonry	The Wheel
Currency	Iron Working	Code of Laws	Writing	Map Making
Mysticism	Mathematics	Literacy	Construction	Astronomy
Invention	University	Navigation	Engineering	Philosophy
Physics	Gunpowder	Magnetism	Metallurgy	Electricity
			Hoover Dam	Electronics

Wonder of the World

Manhattan Project

VITAL STATS

Bonus: Nuclear Weapons
Resources: 600

Obsolete: Never

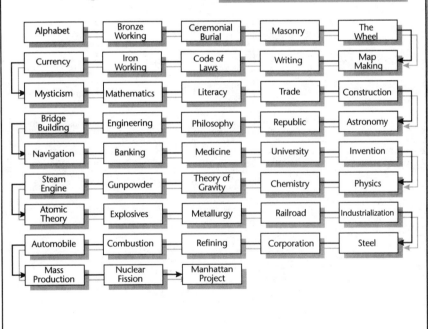

Alphabet	Bronze Working	Ceremonial Burial	Masonry	The Wheel
Currency	Iron Working	Code of Laws	Writing	Map Making
Mysticism	Mathematics	Literacy	Trade	Construction
Bridge Building	Engineering	Philosophy	Republic	Astronomy
Navigation	Banking	Medicine	University	Invention
Steam Engine	Gunpowder	Theory of Gravity	Chemistry	Physics
Atomic Theory	Explosives	Metallurgy	Railroad	Industrialization
Automobile	Combustion	Refining	Corporation	Steel
Mass Production	Nuclear Fission	Manhattan Project		

Wonder of the World

SETI Program

VITAL STATS

Bonus: Knowledge +50%
Resources: 600

Obsolete: Never

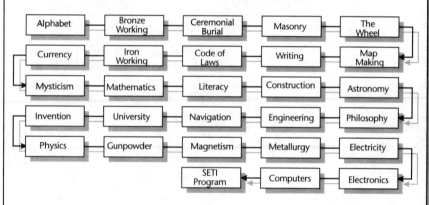

Alphabet	Bronze Working	Ceremonial Burial	Masonry	The Wheel
Currency	Iron Working	Code of Laws	Writing	Map Making
Mysticism	Mathematics	Literacy	Construction	Astronomy
Invention	University	Navigation	Engineering	Philosophy
Physics	Gunpowder	Magnetism	Metallurgy	Electricity
		SETI Program	Computers	Electronics

Wonder of the World

Women's Suffrage

VITAL STATS

Bonus:-1 Unhappy for units away
from home
Resources: 600

Obsolete: Never

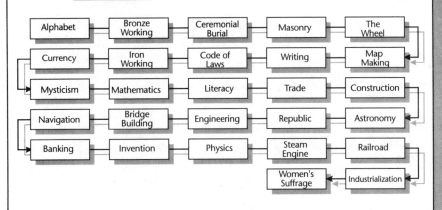

Alphabet	Bronze Working	Ceremonial Burial	Masonry	The Wheel
Currency	Iron Working	Code of Laws	Writing	Map Making
Mysticism	Mathematics	Literacy	Trade	Construction
Navigation	Bridge Building	Engineering	Republic	Astronomy
Banking	Invention	Physics	Steam Engine	Railroad
			Women's Suffrage	Industrialization

Wonder of the World

United Nations

VITAL STATS

Bonus: Other civilizations
offer peace
Resources: 600

Obsolete: Never

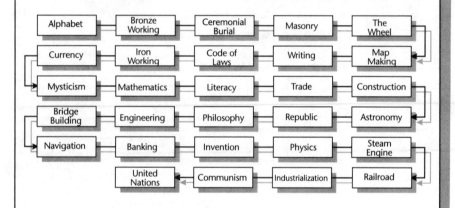

Alphabet	Bronze Working	Ceremonial Burial	Masonry	The Wheel
Currency	Iron Working	Code of Laws	Writing	Map Making
Mysticism	Mathematics	Literacy	Trade	Construction
Bridge Building	Engineering	Philosophy	Republic	Astronomy
Navigation	Banking	Invention	Physics	Steam Engine
United Nations	Communism	Industrialization	Railroad	

Civilization's Military Units

Because many strategies within each simulation will involve the use of a strong military for either offensive or defensive purposes, it is vital for any civilization to be supported by a strong military, which you must begin to develop immediately at the start of the game.

Each of the military unit charts depicts the knowledges needed to build different types of military units.

Once again, it is important to note that once each knowledge is acquired by a civilization, it does not have to be acquired again by each city within the civilization. Thus, as you take part in a simulation, you should keep track of which knowledges your scientists have already acquired (by checking with the Science Advisor).

Building a Military Based Upon Acquired Knowledge

When you are choosing which type(s) of military unit(s) to build, you must first determine which knowledges your civilization has acquired. This will suggest which units you are capable of building. Then you should check the Vital Stats chart that accompanies each military unit chart, to determine that military unit's Attack Strength, Defense Strength, Movement Capabilities, and its Cost in Resources (to build).

To find out which military units (and City Improvements) can be built by your civilization at any time, double-click on the Change button in the City screen of any city within your empire, and the Change menu, listing all of the available military units (and City Improvements), will be displayed.

The higher a unit's Attack, Defense, and Movement values are, the more powerful that unit will be. However, units with high values also cost more resources and will take longer to build.

As we've said, an entire civilization (with all of its cities combined) can build only one of each Wonder of the World. The entire civilization also gets the benefit of knowledge advances made by each city's scientists. Individual cities within the civilization can each build one of every City Improvement. Each city also can create as many of each military unit, and as many Diplomats and Caravan units, as it can maintain.

Diplomats and Caravans Are Non-Military Units

Diplomats and Caravans are not listed within this section; however, Diplomats can be used to assist the military in overthrowing a foreign city, and Caravans can offer support to those cities building Wonders of the World.

To create a Diplomat unit, both the Alphabet and Writing are required. To create Caravan units, your civilization will need the Alphabet, Bronze Working, Code of Laws, Currency, and Trade.

The Military Units

These charts (presented in alphabetical order) outline the knowledges your empire will have to acquire before each type of military unit can be built. Use these charts during a simulation as a resource for creating winning development strategies for your Scientists.

Military Unit

Armor

VITAL STATS

Attack: 10   Movement: 3
Defense: 5   Resources: 80

Obsolete: Never

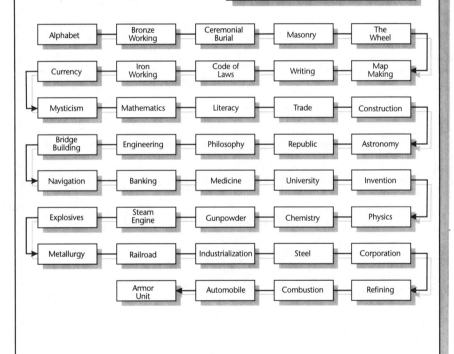

Alphabet	Bronze Working	Ceremonial Burial	Masonry	The Wheel
Currency	Iron Working	Code of Laws	Writing	Map Making
Mysticism	Mathematics	Literacy	Trade	Construction
Bridge Building	Engineering	Philosophy	Republic	Astronomy
Navigation	Banking	Medicine	University	Invention
Explosives	Steam Engine	Gunpowder	Chemistry	Physics
Metallurgy	Railroad	Industrialization	Steel	Corporation
Armor Unit	Automobile	Combustion	Refining	

Military Unit

Artillery

VITAL STATS

Attack: 12   Movement: 2
Defense: 2   Resources: 60

Obsolete: Never

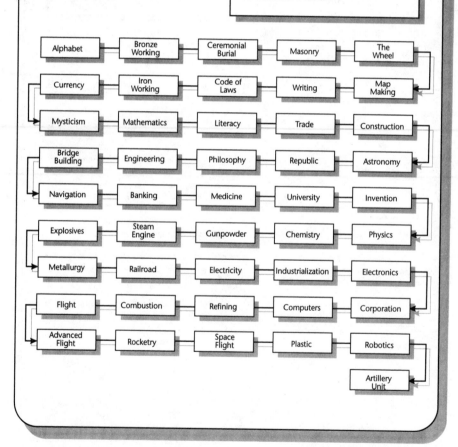

Alphabet	Bronze Working	Ceremonial Burial	Masonry	The Wheel
Currency	Iron Working	Code of Laws	Writing	Map Making
Mysticism	Mathematics	Literacy	Trade	Construction
Bridge Building	Engineering	Philosophy	Republic	Astronomy
Navigation	Banking	Medicine	University	Invention
Explosives	Steam Engine	Gunpowder	Chemistry	Physics
Metallurgy	Railroad	Electricity	Industrialization	Electronics
Flight	Combustion	Refining	Computers	Corporation
Advanced Flight	Rocketry	Space Flight	Plastic	Robotics
				Artillery Unit

Military Unit

Battleship

VITAL STATS

Attack: 18   Movement: 4
Defense: 12   Resources: 160

Obsolete: Never

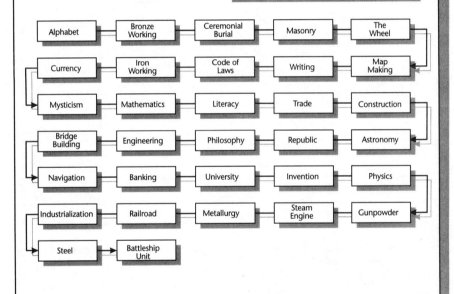

| Alphabet | Bronze Working | Ceremonial Burial | Masonry | The Wheel |

| Currency | Iron Working | Code of Laws | Writing | Map Making |

| Mysticism | Mathematics | Literacy | Trade | Construction |

| Bridge Building | Engineering | Philosophy | Republic | Astronomy |

| Navigation | Banking | University | Invention | Physics |

| Industrialization | Railroad | Metallurgy | Steam Engine | Gunpowder |

| Steel | Battleship Unit |

Military Unit

Bomber

VITAL STATS

Attack: 12   Movement: 8
Defense: 1   Resources: 120

Obsolete: Never

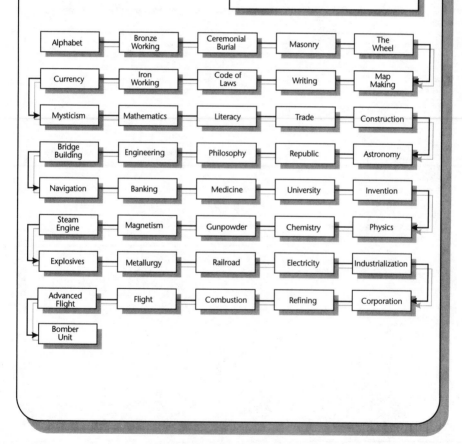

Alphabet	Bronze Working	Ceremonial Burial	Masonry	The Wheel
Currency	Iron Working	Code of Laws	Writing	Map Making
Mysticism	Mathematics	Literacy	Trade	Construction
Bridge Building	Engineering	Philosophy	Republic	Astronomy
Navigation	Banking	Medicine	University	Invention
Steam Engine	Magnetism	Gunpowder	Chemistry	Physics
Explosives	Metallurgy	Railroad	Electricity	Industrialization
Advanced Flight	Flight	Combustion	Refining	Corporation
Bomber Unit				

Military Unit

Cannon

VITAL STATS

Attack: 8   Movement: 1
Defense: 1   Resources: 40

Obsolete: After Artillery

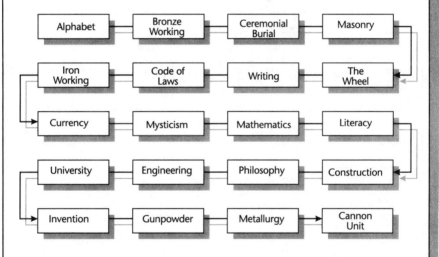

Alphabet	Bronze Working	Ceremonial Burial	Masonry
Iron Working	Code of Laws	Writing	The Wheel
Currency	Mysticism	Mathematics	Literacy
University	Engineering	Philosophy	Construction
Invention	Gunpowder	Metallurgy	Cannon Unit

Military Unit

Carrier

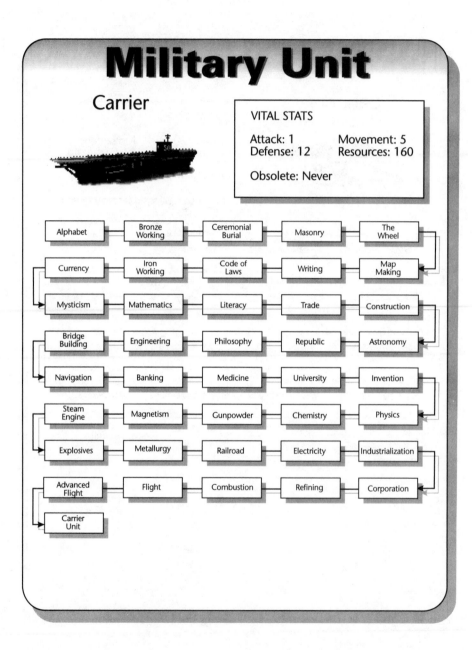

VITAL STATS

Attack: 1   Movement: 5
Defense: 12   Resources: 160

Obsolete: Never

Alphabet	Bronze Working	Ceremonial Burial	Masonry	The Wheel
Currency	Iron Working	Code of Laws	Writing	Map Making
Mysticism	Mathematics	Literacy	Trade	Construction
Bridge Building	Engineering	Philosophy	Republic	Astronomy
Navigation	Banking	Medicine	University	Invention
Steam Engine	Magnetism	Gunpowder	Chemistry	Physics
Explosives	Metallurgy	Railroad	Electricity	Industrialization
Advanced Flight	Flight	Combustion	Refining	Corporation
Carrier Unit				

Military Unit

Catapult

VITAL STATS

Attack: 6   Movement: 1
Defense: 1   Resources: 40

Obsolete: After Cannon

| Alphabet | → | Masonry | → | Mathematics | → | Catapult Unit |

Military Unit

Cavalry

VITAL STATS

Attack: 2   Movement: 2
Defense: 1   Resources: 20

Obsolete: After Riflemen

| Horseback Riding | → | Cavalry Unit |

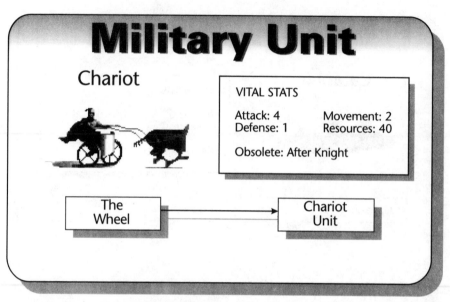

Military Unit

Chariot

VITAL STATS

Attack: 4   Movement: 2
Defense: 1   Resources: 40

Obsolete: After Knight

The Wheel → Chariot Unit

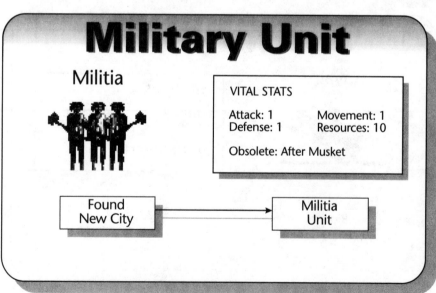

Military Unit

Militia

VITAL STATS

Attack: 1   Movement: 1
Defense: 1   Resources: 10

Obsolete: After Musket

Found New City → Militia Unit

Military Unit

Cruiser

VITAL STATS

Attack: 6   Movement: 6
Defense: 6   Resources: 80

Obsolete: Never

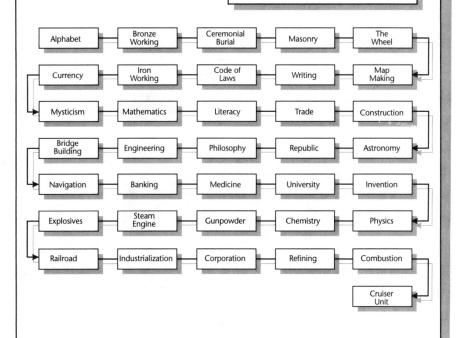

Military Unit

Fighter

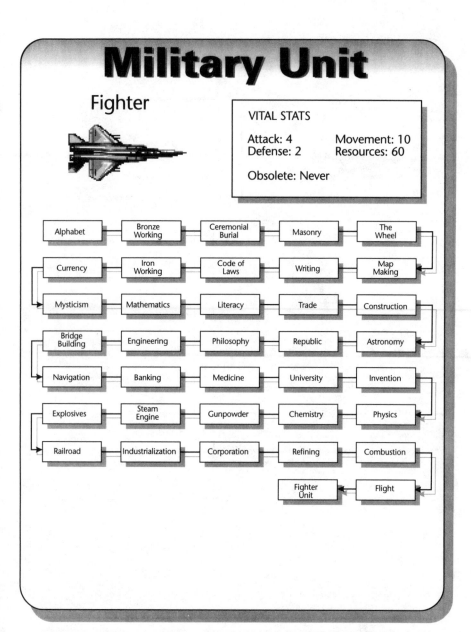

VITAL STATS

Attack: 4 Movement: 10
Defense: 2 Resources: 60

Obsolete: Never

Alphabet	Bronze Working	Ceremonial Burial	Masonry	The Wheel
Currency	Iron Working	Code of Laws	Writing	Map Making
Mysticism	Mathematics	Literacy	Trade	Construction
Bridge Building	Engineering	Philosophy	Republic	Astronomy
Navigation	Banking	Medicine	University	Invention
Explosives	Steam Engine	Gunpowder	Chemistry	Physics
Railroad	Industrialization	Corporation	Refining	Combustion
			Fighter Unit	Flight

Military Unit

Frigate

VITAL STATS

Attack: 2   Movement: 3
Defense: 2   Resources: 40

Obsolete: After Transport

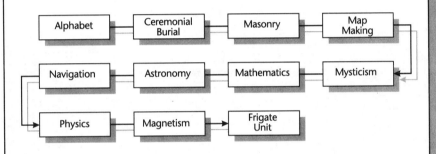

Alphabet	→	Ceremonial Burial	→	Masonry	→	Map Making
Navigation	→	Astronomy	→	Mathematics	→	Mysticism
Physics	→	Magnetism	→	Frigate Unit		

Military Unit

Ironclad

VITAL STATS

Attack: 4   Movement: 4
Defense: 4   Resources: 60

Obsolete: After Cruiser

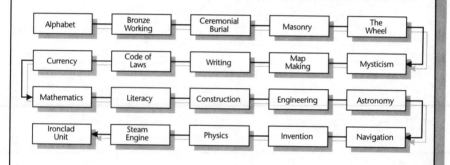

Alphabet	Bronze Working	Ceremonial Burial	Masonry	The Wheel
Currency	Code of Laws	Writing	Map Making	Mysticism
Mathematics	Literacy	Construction	Engineering	Astronomy
Ironclad Unit	Steam Engine	Physics	Invention	Navigation

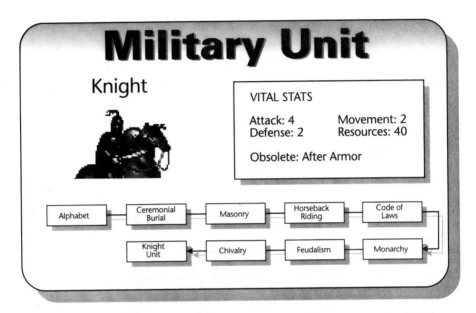

Military Unit

Knight

VITAL STATS

Attack: 4   Movement: 2
Defense: 2   Resources: 40

Obsolete: After Armor

Alphabet → Ceremonial Burial → Masonry → Horseback Riding → Code of Laws

Knight Unit ← Chivalry ← Feudalism ← Monarchy

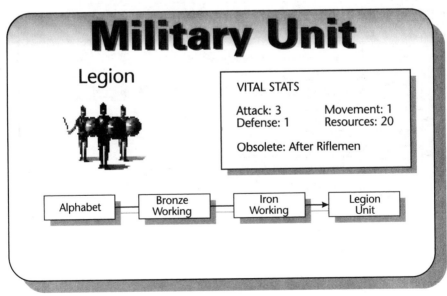

Military Unit

Legion

VITAL STATS

Attack: 3   Movement: 1
Defense: 1   Resources: 20

Obsolete: After Riflemen

Alphabet → Bronze Working → Iron Working → Legion Unit

Military Unit

Mechanized Infantry

VITAL STATS

Attack: 6   Movement: 3
Defense: 6   Resources: 50

Obsolete: Never

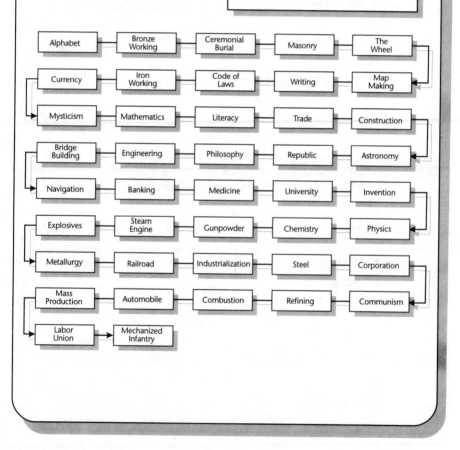

Alphabet	Bronze Working	Ceremonial Burial	Masonry	The Wheel
Currency	Iron Working	Code of Laws	Writing	Map Making
Mysticism	Mathematics	Literacy	Trade	Construction
Bridge Building	Engineering	Philosophy	Republic	Astronomy
Navigation	Banking	Medicine	University	Invention
Explosives	Steam Engine	Gunpowder	Chemistry	Physics
Metallurgy	Railroad	Industrialization	Steel	Corporation
Mass Production	Automobile	Combustion	Refining	Communism
Labor Union	Mechanized Infantry			

Military Unit

Musketeers

VITAL STATS

Attack: 2   Movement: 1
Defense: 3   Resources: 30

Obsolete: After Riflemen

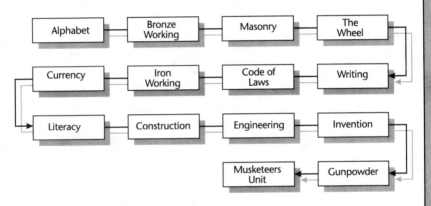

Alphabet	Bronze Working	Masonry	The Wheel
Currency	Iron Working	Code of Laws	Writing
Literacy	Construction	Engineering	Invention
	Musketeers Unit		Gunpowder

Military Unit

Nuclear

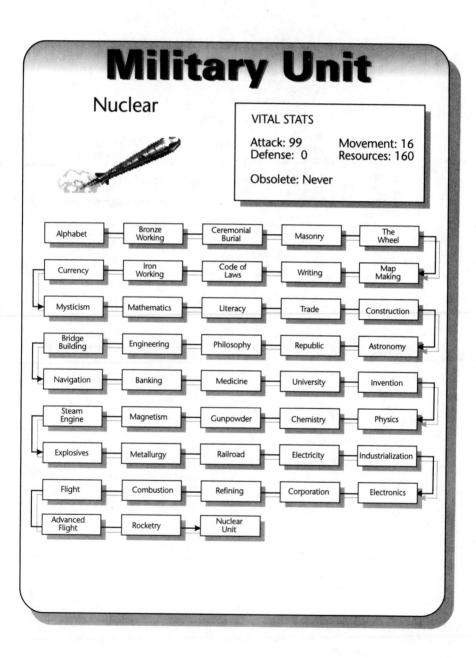

VITAL STATS

Attack: 99   Movement: 16
Defense: 0   Resources: 160

Obsolete: Never

Alphabet	Bronze Working	Ceremonial Burial	Masonry	The Wheel
Currency	Iron Working	Code of Laws	Writing	Map Making
Mysticism	Mathematics	Literacy	Trade	Construction
Bridge Building	Engineering	Philosophy	Republic	Astronomy
Navigation	Banking	Medicine	University	Invention
Steam Engine	Magnetism	Gunpowder	Chemistry	Physics
Explosives	Metallurgy	Railroad	Electricity	Industrialization
Flight	Combustion	Refining	Corporation	Electronics
Advanced Flight	Rocketry	Nuclear Unit		

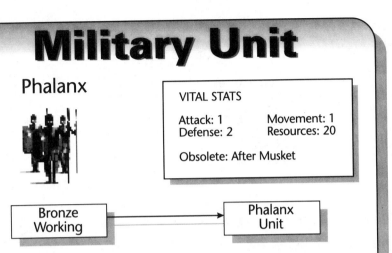

Military Unit

Phalanx

VITAL STATS

Attack: 1   Movement: 1
Defense: 2   Resources: 20

Obsolete: After Musket

Bronze Working → Phalanx Unit

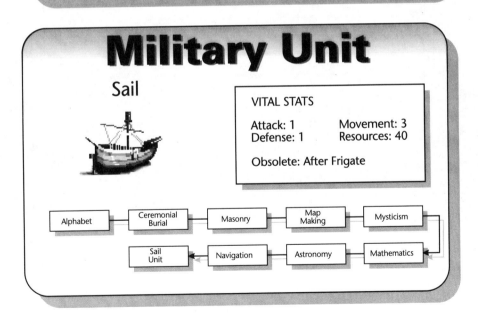

Military Unit

Sail

VITAL STATS

Attack: 1   Movement: 3
Defense: 1   Resources: 40

Obsolete: After Frigate

Alphabet → Ceremonial Burial → Masonry → Map Making → Mysticism

Sail Unit ← Navigation ← Astronomy ← Mathematics

Military Unit

Riflemen

VITAL STATS

Attack: 3   Movement: 1
Defense: 5   Resources: 30

Obsolete: Never

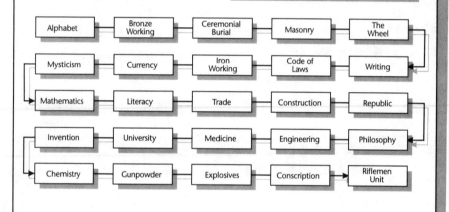

Alphabet	Bronze Working	Ceremonial Burial	Masonry	The Wheel
Mysticism	Currency	Iron Working	Code of Laws	Writing
Mathematics	Literacy	Trade	Construction	Republic
Invention	University	Medicine	Engineering	Philosophy
Chemistry	Gunpowder	Explosives	Conscription	Riflemen Unit

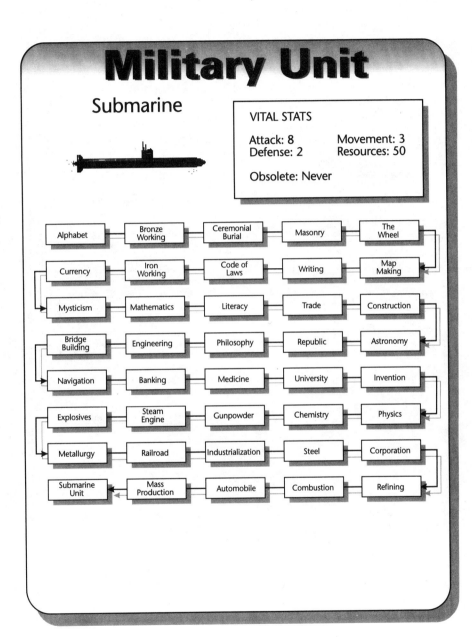

Military Unit

Submarine

VITAL STATS

Attack: 8   Movement: 3
Defense: 2   Resources: 50

Obsolete: Never

Alphabet	Bronze Working	Ceremonial Burial	Masonry	The Wheel
Currency	Iron Working	Code of Laws	Writing	Map Making
Mysticism	Mathematics	Literacy	Trade	Construction
Bridge Building	Engineering	Philosophy	Republic	Astronomy
Navigation	Banking	Medicine	University	Invention
Explosives	Steam Engine	Gunpowder	Chemistry	Physics
Metallurgy	Railroad	Industrialization	Steel	Corporation
Submarine Unit	Mass Production	Automobile	Combustion	Refining

Military Unit

Transport

VITAL STATS	
Attack: 0	Movement: 4
Defense: 3	Resources: 50
Obsolete: Never	

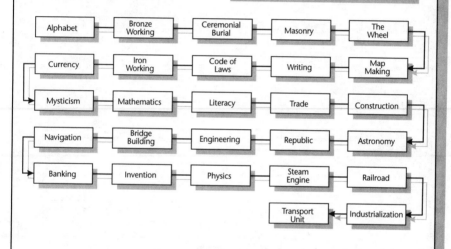

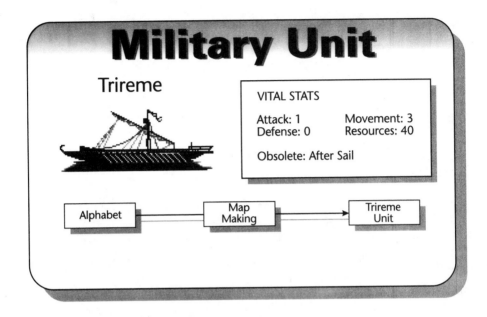

The Next Step Is Playing

Thus far, this book has offered an overview of Civilization, tutorials, and strategies to get you started playing your own simulations. The next step is for you to experience firsthand what this game has to offer by playing for yourself.

For more Civilization secrets, turn to Chapter 10, which offers information on how to "cheat."

Chapter 10

Learning to Cheat

Anyone who follows politics knows that not all politicians are always on the up-and-up. What does that say for leaders of great empires?

Getting Ahead as a Leader

As you probably already know, Civilization is a challenging game that requires you to juggle many responsibilities as you strive to expand your empire. Maybe you've wished that Civilization was a bit less challenging. There are a *number* of methods of cheating—we'll talk about seven of them here.

Two of these methods require the use of a modem to download short utility programs written by dedicated Civilization players and made available (free of charge) through various on-line services. The other methods of cheating can be done using keyboard commands, but only in certain (specified) versions of the game.

Cheating in Civilization Versions 1 and 2

In the early versions of Civilization (versions 1 and 2 only), MicroProse Software included a built-in cheat mode within the program. If you are using either of those early versions of Civilization, try holding down the left Shift key and then pressing: **1 2 3 4 5 6 7 8 9 0 t**.

You will enter a special "debug" mode, which was taken out of the game in later versions. While you're in this debug mode, double-click on the small map portion of the Main Game screen and you'll instantly see a view of the entire world—even areas you have not yet explored—including the locations of all rival cities!

You'll also be able to enter the City screens of rival cities and sell off their improvements and Wonders of the World.

While still in debug mode, try pressing the various function keys (F1 through F10 on your keyboard) and check out what they do. For example, press F7 to see how well rival civilizations are developing, F8 to see a line graph charting your progress, and F9 to get information on the terrain squares that comprise your continent.

Placing a "Hex" on Civilization: For Programmers Only

When you save a game in Civilization, a CIVIL#.SVE file is created. (The symbol # here represents a number between 0 and 9, which will be inserted automatically in place of the symbol.)

Before proceeding, be sure you are very familiar with the use of hex editors. *This method is for programmers only.*

One player has discovered that if you use a hex editor (such as the Disk Editor in Norton Utilities, or another hex editor in some similar software package) you can modify a saved game and change the amount of money in your treasury.

This trick involves converting the amount of money you have into a hexadecimal numerical value, and then altering the *bytes* (i.e., 1234 becomes 3412 and ABCD becomes CDAB).

The hex numerical value can be found within the CIVIL#.SVE file somewhere around offset 135h-150h. Change this number, and you will create a whole new game play experience (by adding funds to your treasury) from your saved game data.

Be sure to make a backup of the CIVIL#.SVE file before tampering with it. Then, if you make a mistake, the original data file can be used, and the game can continue.

Civilization Time Travel

This cheating method requires a short (only 9359 bytes long) utility program called CIVDTE.EXE, which allows you to *change the date of any saved game file.*

Installing CIVDTE.EXE

You can download CIVDTE.ZIP (as CIVDTE.EXE is known in its compressed state) from one of the on-line services (such as CompuServe, America OnLine, or the MicroProse BBS) and then use a decompression program to decompress the file.

See Chapter 3 on Installing Civilization for more information on decompression programs and techniques.

Place the CIVDTE.EXE file in the directory that contains the Civilization program. (If the software is on your hard disk, it will be in the C:\MPS\CIV subdirectory.)

Getting to CIVDTE.EXE's Documentation

To get a brief explanation of how this program works, type **CIVDTE** and press Enter.

Using CIVDTE.EXE

Suppose you're taking part in a simulation and you're about to conquer the world and reach Alpha Centauri—*but* the year is *2070 AD* (which means that the program will *terminate* in just thirty years, if you're playing at the Chieftain level).

Using the CIVDTE.EXE utility, you can save the game data by accessing Civilization's Game pull-down menu and selecting the Save Game option.

When you save the game, you must know *where* the game data was saved (there are ten possibilities: CIVIL0.SVE through CIVIL9.SVE).

Once the game data is saved,

1. Enter the directory where the Civilization game is located (on a hard disk, the default directory is C:\MPS\CIV).

2. At the DOS prompt, type **CIVDTE** followed by:

   A. The filename (**CIVIL#.SVE**, with the # symbol replaced by the correct number).

   B. The year in which you wish to restart the simulation.

When you type in the year to which you wish to change, use *positive* numbers for *AD* dates or *negative* numbers for *BC* dates. Thus, if the game you want to modify was saved as CIVIL1.SVE and you wish to change the year to 500 AD, you should type: **CIVDTE CIVIL1.SVE 500** and press Enter.

Keep in mind that everything about the game will be exactly the same—*only the date will have changed.*

Within seconds, the file will be modified and you can reload Civilization, then load in the game data stored in CIVIL1.SVE. To return to Civilization,

3. Select Load a Saved Game and restart your simulation, just as you would normally.

Now, instead of the year being 2070 AD, it could be 100 AD, or any other date you choose, which will allow you to finish (and presumably win) your simulation.

Giving Your Civilization Megabucks

Game player Richard Lawrence has written a utility program called CC.EXE (Civilization Cheat), which simply adds money ($30,000, to be exact) to your empire's treasury.

CC.EXE can be downloaded from the various on-line services, as mentioned before. (You may also have to use a public domain or shareware decompression utility to convert the CC.ZIP file you download into the CC.EXE file.) Place CC.EXE in the directory on your hard disk that contains Civilization (usually C:\MPS\CIV).

Using CC.EXE

To adjust your empire's treasury, save the game data of the current simulation as usual and Quit the game. Let's say that Civilization named the game data file CIVIL1.SVE and let's use that file name in our example.

To make the treasury $30,000 within the simulation saved as CIVIL1.SVE,

1. At the C:\MPS\CIV\ prompt, type:
   CC CIVILA.BAK CIVIL1.SVE.

2. Press Enter.

In the command line you typed (above), CC executed the program, CIVILA.BAK was the name you gave a *new* backup file (in which the old, unaltered game data was stored), and CIVIL1.SVE was the name of the saved game data file you wanted (in this example) to alter. You could have named the backup file anything (less than eight characters long), as long as you used the .BAK extension.

3. Now, reload CIVIL1.SVE by using the Load Saved Game option in Civilization.

You'll notice that a very large deposit has been made to your treasury. Now, you can purchase any Wonders of the World that are available, or any other units you wish.

Getting CC Help

For quick help with this program, at the DOS prompt, type **CC ?**.

Happy spending!

Strategies to Make Playing Easier

This section discusses a few bugs in Civilization that can actually be used to make some aspects of playing the game a little easier.

Flying Bomber Units

Once you have created Bomber units, fly them over water during their first turn in operation and then place them on Sentry duty—the Bomber units will sit there until they are removed from Sentry duty and reactivated.

When you're ready, you can send a Carrier unit to pick up the Bombers. That will remove them from Sentry duty and make them into active units, which you can use to launch an attack.

When a unit is on Sentry duty, its purpose is to defend itself against attack, not initiate one.

Improving Your Military

If you want to improve your military forces without having to earn the prerequisite knowledges, you can use Diplomats to steal Conscription and Explosives from rival empires, then use those technologies to build more advanced military units without ever having to discover Gunpowder yourself.

Stealing Knowledges and Wonders of the World

If a rival civilization is technologically ahead of yours and is developing a Wonder of the World that you wish to acquire, engage in a military attack and capture the city that is developing that wonder. Once you have taken over the rival city, the wonder (which was already in development) will continue to be built, but now it will belong to *your* civilization, even if you have not made the technological advances that normally would have been needed.

"Cheating" to Learn

Playing Civilization can be especially fun when your strategies and leadership abilities prove to be successful. Providing yourself with a $30,000 treasury increase—or using any of the other "cheating" techniques outlined in this chapter—will allow you to develop different types of Civilization experience.

Experiment with different aspects of the game; you'll find your empire's capacity to grow through building is now almost limitless.

Chapter 11

Using the Keyboard Commands

Let's face it—with the popularity of Microsoft Windows and many graphics-based software applications, the computer *mouse* has become a popular, useful, and relatively inexpensive accessory. Despite this, there are still plenty of PC users (including some using laptop and notebook computers) who do not have access to a computer mouse. This chapter will explain how to play Civilization using the keyboard.

Mouse users can also take advantage of keyboard shortcuts while playing Civilization; however, mouse and keyboard entry should not be combined within a specific command in the game.

To play with the keyboard only, you're going to have to *remember* many more commands in order to accomplish what might be simple point-and-click procedures if you were using a mouse.

When you make menu selections (from the Main Game screen's pull-down menus) be sure either to use just keyboard commands or just mouse clicks, *not both*.

Moving Around the Main Game Screen

Most of the game takes place on the Main Game screen. You can move quickly around the main map area (in the center of the screen) by pressing the Tab key to generate a cursor, then holding down the Shift key in conjunction with the directional arrow keys (Up, Down, Left, and Right) to move in any direction you wish.

Activating Specific Units

To activate a unit within this main map area, simply place the cursor on that unit (by using the Shift key in combination with directional arrows) and then press Enter.

Accessing the Game's City Screens

When you want to access the City screen for a specific city, place the cursor on the city square icon (containing a number) and press Enter. The City screen for that city will then appear.

Accessing the Game's Pull-Down Menus

As you know, at the Main Game screen you can gain access to various pull-down menus that work within the game.

The *menu bar*, located at the top of the Main Game screen, offers the following options:

- Game
- Orders
- Advisors
- World
- Civilopedia

To access any of these pull-down menus without using a mouse, hold down the ALT key and simultaneously press the *first letter* of the menu option you wish to select. (For example, press ALT+G for the Game pull-down menu or press ALT+O to access the menu options in the Orders pull-down menu.)

After you select the specific pull-down menu you need, further options may be displayed. One option will be highlighted. Use the arrow keys on the keyboard (on some keyboards, these are part of the numeric keypad), to move up or down the list of menu options. When the option you wish to choose is highlighted, press Enter to select it.

Fortifying or Activating Units from the Main Game Screen

An active unit can be fortified (or placed on Sentry duty) by first selecting the Orders menu and then selecting either of these two options. To reactivate a specific unit that is fortified or on Sentry duty,

1. Press A (for Activate) and use the directional arrow keys to move the cursor around the screen to select the unit you wish to activate.

2. When the correct unit is selected (using the cursor), press Enter to activate that unit.

Controlling the City Screen with Keyboard Commands

There are graphic icons in the City screens that you can use to activate certain game play options. Each icon is labeled with a name. To activate these icons without a mouse, press the first letter of the icon's name. To activate the Change icon, for example, press C. On the City screen you would press the following:

C   Change

B   Buy

R   Rename

E   Exit

V   View

M   Map

H   Happy

I   Info (information)

P   People (to create elite citizens)

S   Sell a City Improvement

Creating Entertainers, Taxmen, and Scientists

Within the City screen you also can assign specific members of the population to jobs—for example, you assign jobs to regular workers, or you can make citizens into Entertainers, then into Taxmen and finally Scientists. Normally, to convert a normal citizen into an Entertainer, you would use the mouse to double-click on a wheat symbol, which symbolizes farmland and the farm people who work the land. Wheat symbols can be found on the small map in the center of the City screen. To do the same using just the keyboard commands,

1. Press **P** to activate the cursor, which will then appear in the map area.

2. Using the directional arrows on your keyboard (or the numeric keypad), move the cursor to the wheat symbols on the map.

3. Press Enter to convert a normal citizen into an Entertainer.

Once an Entertainer is created, it can then be transformed into a Taxman and then Scientist, or back into a normal citizen. After creating the Entertainer, you will notice that the population roster in the upper-left portion of the City screen has changed—now it displays fewer regular citizens and one additional Entertainer.

If you were using a mouse, you would double-click on the Elite Citizen icon in the population roster to change the Entertainer into a Taxman.

Near the population roster, starting from the left side of the screen, will be numbers identifying each elite citizen. To convert an Entertainer into a Taxman,

1. Press the number on the keyboard that corresponds to the Entertainer you want to convert.

2. Press the same number a second time to convert that same citizen from a Taxman to a Scientist.

Selling Improvements and Wonders of the World

In the upper-right corner of the City screen is the list of City Improvements and Wonders of the World that city has acquired or built. Next to each improvement or wonder is a small circle icon—this is the Sell icon for that improvement or wonder. If you were using a mouse, you would double-click on the small circle icon to sell the corresponding improvement or wonder. To sell a listed City Improvement or Wonder of the World using the keyboard,

1. Press **S** to convert the listing into a standard menu with a highlighted bar.

2. Using the directional arrow keys, highlight the improvement or wonder you wish to sell.

3. Press Enter.

4. A Yes/No dialog box will appear, which will also note the value of the improvement or wonder you are planning to sell. If you select Yes (by pressing Y on the keyboard) the improvement will disappear from the list and your civilization's treasury will increase accordingly. If you select No (by pressing N), the sale will not happen.

If the word "More" appears at the end of the list of improvements or wonders, indicating that the list is too long to fit within the window, press Shift+M (More) to see the rest of the list.

Using the Function Keys

Each of the function keys (F1 through F10) on the keyboard perform specific tasks within the simulation. Instead of accessing individual pull-down menus and then highlighting your specific choices, you can use the function keys to save time and keystrokes. The following is a list of those commands or features that can be activated using the function keys:

F1	City Status
F2	Military Advisor
F3	Intelligence Advisor
F4	Attitude Advisor
F5	Trade Advisor
F6	Science Advisor

F7   Wonders of the World (acquired)

F8   Top 5 Cities

F9   Current Civilization Score

F10   World Map

Changing the Tax and Luxury Rates

You can change the Tax Rate or Luxury Rate during a simulation by accessing the Game pull-down menu and then selecting the Tax rate or Luxury Rate menu choice.

An alternate method for adjusting these rates quickly is to press + to adjust the Tax Rate and − to adjust the Luxury Rate. A menu will appear then, listing the various values to which the Tax Rate or Luxury Rate can be adjusted. Use the directional arrows to highlight your choice and then press Enter to actually change the rate.

Saving Game Data Fast

If you have chosen to deactivate the Autosave option, or if you wish to save the game data at a specific point, you can access the Game pull-down menu and select the Save Game option *or* you can press Shift+S to quickly save the game data without dealing with the menus.

Other Helpful
Keyboard Shortcut Commands

The following additional keyboard shortcuts can be used even if you're primarily relying on a mouse to interact with the game.

Centering the Game Screen Around the Active Unit

From the Main Game screen, you can press C to center the main map around the currently active unit.

Activating the Main Game Screen's Cursor

To activate the cursor in the main map area, press the Tab key. Then you can use the directional arrow keys to move the cursor.

Getting On-Screen Help

To activate the on-screen Help menu, press ALT+H.

Exiting the Game Quickly

To Quit the game (without saving the game data) press ALT+Q.

Moving the Active Unit

To move the active unit, use the directional arrow keys.

Commands Under the Orders Menu

When you activate the Orders pull-down menu, you can activate any of the following options by pressing single letters as opposed to moving the highlighted bar to the appropriate menu option. First, however, you must access the orders menu by pressing Alt+O.

One-Letter Commands

The following list of one-letter commands can be activated from the Orders pull-down menu:

Spacebar	No Orders
Shift+P	Pillage
S	Sentry Duty
U	Unload Ship
W	Wait

I	Agricultural Improvement
F	Fortify
R	Build Railroad
P	Clear Pollution
Shift+D	Disband a Unit
B	Found a New City
G	GoTo
H	Home City
M	Industrial Improvement

Making Tracks with the GoTo Command

The GoTo command is handy when you have a specific destination (across multiple squares) in mind for a unit, that will take multiple turns to reach. Use the GoTo command for this, and you won't have to keep moving the unit manually as each turn passes. To use the GoTo option,

1. Activate the unit you wish to move.

2. Once the unit is flashing (active), press G. The Active unit will continue to flash; however, the box cursor will appear.

3. Using the directional arrows, move the cursor to the destination you want the Active unit to reach.

4. With the cursor at that location (the unit will remain in its original location) press Enter.

As each turn now passes, the computer will assist you by automatically determining what route the unit will take and moving the unit over the maximum number of terrain squares allowable, until that unit reaches the destination you have selected.

Playing Civilization without a mouse does not change the way you actually play the game; however, it does require you to learn additional commands in order to quickly move around the game and make the fast decisions necessary to your success.

The next chapter, Chapter 12, will explain Civilization scoring and provide some inside tips for a winning score.

Chapter 12

High Scorin' Civilization Fun

During a simulation, you can measure your progress in a number of ways—funds in your treasury, military conquests, scientific developments, or your point score. At any time during a game, you can access the Civilization Score option found under the World pull-down menu on the Main Game screen. The Civilization Score display will provide you with:

- The total number of citizens in your tribe

- The Wonders of the World your tribe has obtained

- The number of bonus points you have received for each peaceful turn

- The total Civilization Score you have earned thus far

Understanding the Civilization Score Display

The Civilization Score is made up of a number of components, which will be described in this chapter. A typical score screen is shown in Figure 12.1.

Getting Points for the Size and Happiness of Your Population

The first component is a count of your civilization's entire population combined with award points based on the status of each citizen. You can expect to receive:

2 Points   for each happy citizen

1 Point   for each content citizen

1 Point   for each elite citizen

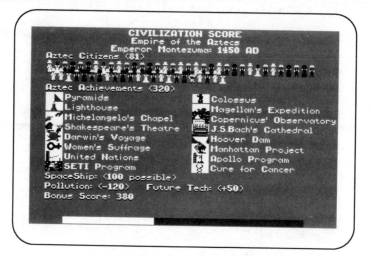

Figure 12.1: The Civilization Score screen at the end of a simulation

Scoring for Obtaining Wonders of the World

Next, the computer will evaluate the number of Wonders of the World your civilization has acquired and award you:

   20 Points   for each Wonder of the World

With twenty-one potential wonders available, that's 420 potential points available to earn.

Extra Points for Peaceful Turns

You will also be awarded:

   3 Points   for each peaceful turn

A peaceful turn is one in which your civilization experienced no attacks or war-like actions. Later in the game, after you have conquered the majority of other civilizations and your empire is working toward colonizing space, you should be able to rack up a large number of peaceful turn points, since there will be few rival tribes remaining to fight.

Extra Points for Obtaining Future Technologies

In the very late stages of the game, there are a variety of Future Technologies available for your scientists to acquire. They are worth:

5 Points   for each Future Technology

Gaining Points through Space Travel

Colonizing space is another way to build up points. Your empire will receive:

50 Points   for each 10,000 space colonists that successfully arrive at Alpha Centauri

There's also a Space Travel Bonus, which is based on the number of colonists that land on Alpha Centauri compared to the initial Probability of Success (which was displayed when the spaceship was launched). The Space Bonus formula is *points received for the number of colonists that landed* multiplied by *the Probability of Success of the mission.*

Thus, if 40,000 colonists reach Alpha Centauri, you receive 200 points. Those 200 points multiplied by a 90% Probability of Success rating results in a Space Travel Bonus of 180 points (200 x .9 = 180).

Losing Points through Pollution

While colonizing space can be a great booster of points, not being able to control pollution back on your home planet can cause serious penalties in points. When your score is tabulated,

10 Points   will be deducted for each terrain square containing pollution

Dealing with Pollution

The easiest way to clean up a polluted terrain square is with a group of Settlers. Move the Settlers onto the polluted square and select the Clear Pollution option (P) from the Orders pull-down menu. It will take four turns for Settlers to clean up a polluted square. Until the pollution is cleaned up, food production for that square will decrease. Building a Recycling Center, a Hydro Plant, Mass Transit, Nuclear Power Plant, and/or the Hoover Dam Wonder of the World will also help to reduce the risk of pollution within that city.

If pollution is not controlled within your empire, and nine or more terrain squares become polluted, your entire planet will begin to experience the effects of global warming. These effects may result in a change of terrain squares from Grasslands and Plains to Swamps (or worse).

Figure 12.2: Notice the Pollution icon within the Information window of this City screen.

Causes of Pollution

There are several causes of pollution (Factories and Manufacturing Plants are just two examples), all of which begin to come into play in the middle and later stages of a simulation.

Some Strategies for Building Points

You can take advantage of some of the scoring rules to build a higher score, by keeping in mind the strategies presented here.

Building Points Near the End of the Game

The best time to earn plenty of points is in the final stages of the game. When your empire is about to defeat its final rival on the planet, build up your military forces near that final foe; however, at the same time, cut taxes dramatically, and increase the Luxury Rate.

Now, wait a few turns for these changes to take place. Adjusting the Tax Rate and Luxury Rate in the final turns of the game will convert unhappy or content citizens into happy citizens and earn you the extra points.

Building Points by Keeping the Population Happy

Another strategy is to try to keep your population as happy as possible throughout the simulation, by building those City Improvements and Wonders of the World that boost happiness. Thus, at the end of the game, when the final point score is about to be tabulated, you won't have to do a lot of catch-up work to win the hearts of your population and earn those two-points-per-happy-citizen.

Building Up Future Technologies

Yet another strategy can be implemented once you assign your scientists to develop Future Technologies. Since each Future Technology is worth 5 points, you can increase your scientific efforts by adjusting the Tax Rate to 80% Science—or 90%, or even 100% Science—and allow these Future Technology advances to be created quickly before the simulation ends.

Conquering-the-World Bonus Points

If you manage to build a military strong enough to conquer all of the rival empires on your planet, you will receive a 1,000 point bonus for conquering the world and becoming the world leader by the year 2000 AD.

In addition, you'll earn 2 more points per turn if you conquer the world *before* 2000 AD (but you'll lose 2 points per turn if you conquer the world *after* 2000 AD, so if your goal is world domination, it's a good idea to achieve that as soon as possible).

Overall, at the end of a simulation, your goal is to earn over 1,000 points; however, the higher the score, the better. Thus, if you manage to colonize space *and* conquer the world, chances are you'll receive a very respectable final score.

Comparing Your Success to That of Your Rivals

Following the Civilization Score screen at the end of the simulation, you will see a chart that compares your success (or failure) to that of the rival civilizations on your planet. Along the bottom of the chart is a timeline; each civilization's progress is displayed in the form of a line graph as shown in Figure 12.3.

Comparing Your Success to Historical Leaders

Then you'll see a screen comparing your overall performance to that of well-known, real-life world leaders. Based on your score and the skill level you chose, you could be rated as a leader equivalent to Dan Quayle (the worst possible rating, *and* a total insult in Sid

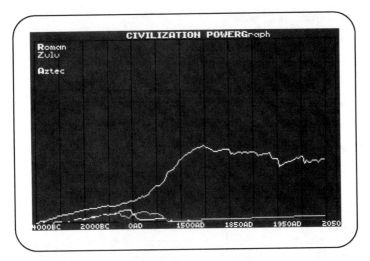

Figure 12.3: A line graph compares your success to that of other civilizations within the simulation

Meier's eyes). Beginning with the worst rating and moving up the scale, you might be compared to:

- Dan Quayle
- Emperor Nero
- Ferdinand Marcos
- Neville Chamberlain
- Louis XVI
- Kaiser Wilhelm
- Erik the Red
- Otto von Bismark
- Simon Bolivar
- Vladimir Lenin
- Charles de Gaulle
- Cleopatra

- Winston Churchill
- Sulayman the Magnificent
- Franklin Roosevelt
- Shogun Tokugawa
- Thomas Jefferson
- King Charlemagne
- Emperor Augustus
- Solomon the Wise (the highest possible rating)

A Few Last Words

Your Civilization score is just another aspect of the game that makes it a challenge. Even after you have developed your own strategies for conquering the world and/or colonizing Alpha Centauri, you can always attempt to discover new strategies to increase your overall point score (without cheating).

Initially, Civilization may seem like an extremely complex and confusing game that takes brain power and time to complete; whatever you do, don't give up and throw the software package into the closet! Instead, spend an hour or two tinkering with a trial-run simulation. Using your imagination along with your ability to define strategies, chances are you will become captivated by Civilization's challenge and originality.

It's no accident that Civilization has won numerous awards within the software industry. Game Player's *PC Entertainment* magazine said it best (when they first reviewed the game) by stating, "Civilization is one if the most novel and entertaining strategy games we've ever seen. The interface is friendly and practical, and the game is sprinkled with delightful graphics and a fine sense of humor. It has all the makings of a classic!"

If you enjoy strategy games that are designed to challenge your mind rather than your fast reflexes, you've made an excellent choice in Civilization. Once you've mastered this game, you might want to check out Sid Meier's Railroad Tycoon (another of MicroProse's best-sellers).

SimCity, SimEarth, SimAnt, and SimLife are also superior simulation programs (from Maxis Software); as are Populous and Populous II (from Electronic Arts).

Caesar (from Impressions Software) is another alternative, if you're looking for an entertaining software package that allows you to build cities and manage a population.

Let the Games Go On

Computers are excellent for word processing and number crunching; however, if you want to spend a few relaxing hours challenging your mind, they can also be an excellent entertainment medium, presenting the work of software developers who are as creative as motion picture producers.

We're living in a wonderful high-tech era. Let the games begin…and may all of your game scores be *high* scores!

Appendix A

Avoiding Bugs and Problems

Civilization is a complex computer program—and, like many programs, it contains a few *bugs* (errors in the programming).

The AutoSave Bug in Early Versions of Civilization

The most obvious bug in Civilization sometimes occurs in the midst of a simulation and causes the computer to *hang* (which means it just stops—you can't save the game data, and you must *reboot*, or restart the computer).

This bug often takes effect when the City screen is displayed and you attempt to use the Change option.

To deal with it in Civilization Versions 1, 2, and 3, an excellent strategy is to leave the Autosave option activated *and* to perform a manual save whenever an important event takes place.

The good news is that the programmers at MicroProse Software have been hard at work attempting to fix this bug. But since the bug has not totally been fixed as of the official release of Civilization Version 4, the easiest way to work around it is to *deactivate* the Instant Advisor option found under the Options pull-down menu that is under the Game menu. This should stop the game from hanging.

Bug-Fixes in Version 5

At the time this book was written, MicroProse had just released Version 5 of Civilization, which—like previous upgrades—was made available for downloading, free of charge, on the various on-line services.

From CompuServe, Prodigy, America OnLine, or the MicroProse BBS, download the file CIVV05.ZIP (and, if necessary, a decompression utility such as PKunzip). Version 5 of Civilization is supposed to include a fix for that pesky bug in the program; however, beta-testers have reported mixed results.

Don't Run Civilization with Memory Resident Programs

In addition to the bug already discussed, players have found that Civilization *does not work* on a computer that is running *memory resident* programs (for example, SideKick). When you start Civilization with a memory resident program already running (or when you later start a memory resident program with Civilization already running), there is a possibility that both programs will *crash*, meaning you'll have to reboot the computer, and choose to run either Civilization *or* the memory resident program.

Pay Attention to System Requirements

Additionally, you should pay attention to the memory requirements listed on the game's packaging—a minimum of 640K RAM (random access memory) is required. If you are running the program in VGA graphics mode, with Sound Blaster drivers and the mouse driver, you're going to require plenty of RAM. If you don't have enough RAM, an error message will appear on screen following the game's title screen. Often, you will be able to continue; however, there is a strong possibility the game's graphic displays will be incomplete. Running the program in EGA mode requires less memory. It is also an option not to use a sound driver and/or the mouse driver, and thus to require less memory.

One Last Bug at the End

One other bug occurs at the end of the simulation, when you are given the option to end the program or to continue to play without the computer keeping score. If you choose to keep playing, do *NOT*

access the Civilization Score option found under the World pull-down menu or by pressing F9, because activating this option could cause the computer to freeze.

To unfreeze the game, try double-clicking the mouse in the Palace area on the left side of the main game screen. This usually works, but not always. You may have to reboot the computer in order to continue.

Stay Out of Turbo Mode

Finally, if your IBM PC-compatible computer has a Turbo mode, be sure that it is turned off before you attempt to run Civilization, or the program may not operate correctly.

Dealing with Other Potential Problems

Assuming that you have the proper system configuration to run Civilization, if the game fails to load or run correctly, contact your local computer software dealer or MicroProse's Technical Support Department. Their telephone number is listed in the game's original manual.

Index

This index uses certain typographical conventions to assist you in finding information. **Boldface** page numbers are references to primary topics and explanations that are emphasized in the text. *Italics* indicate page numbers that reference figures.

The Military Units

Icon	Unit	Attack Strength	Defense Strength	Movement	Resources Required	Advances Required
	Armor	10	5	3	80	Automobile
	Artillery	12	2	2	60	Robotics
	Battleship	18	12	4	160	Steel
	Bomber	12	1	8	120	Advanced Flight
	Cannon	8	1	1	40	Metallurgy
	Carrier	1	12	5	160	Advanced Flight
	Catapult	6	1	1	40	Mathematics
	Cavalry	2	1	2	20	Horseback Riding
	Chariot	4	1	2	40	The Wheel
	Cruiser	6	6	6	80	Combustion
	Fighter	3	3	10	60	Flight
	Frigate	2	2	3	40	Magnetism
	Ironclad	4	4	4	60	Steam Engine